I do not condone the smuggler antics or life-styles of the likeable Steve Lamb and his buddies. Many of them grew up in my neighborhood. As a federal fisheries agent assigned to the national counter-narcotics effort, I was on the other side. In my opinion, Lamb's story is authentic and exemplifies the countless tales I heard while interviewing maritime smugglers in federal prisons around the country. His amazing success in importing tons of marijuana despite endless foul-ups is a fantastic read.

This is a well-written book and a page turner. The U.S. eventually won the drug war at sea, but at a tremendous cost.

—Charles M. Fuss, Jr., author of
Sea of Grass: The Maritime Drug War,
1970-1990
(Naval Institute Press, 1996)

THE
SMUGGLER'S
GHOST

THE
SMUGGLER'S
GHOST

by Steve Lamb
with Diane Marcou

Foreword by Everett S. Rice
Sheriff of Pinellas County, Fla. (ret.)

Sirena Press
Madeira Beach, Florida

For information:

www.TheSmugglersGhost.com

ISBN 978-0-9819432-0-6

Cover and Book Design
theMurmaid ᵗᵐ
for Sirena Press

Printed in the United States of America

First Edition

This story relates actual events in the life of Stephen Lamb as remembered by him. However, some names and descriptive details of some characters have been altered to respect their privacy.

Cover photos, Steve Lamb, 1970s

FOREWORD

NAME: Stephen Garrett Lamb

DOB: November 17, 1952

CITY: St.Pete Beach **COUNTY**: Pinellas **STATE**: Fla.

For years, this was how I kept up with Steve Lamb. In law enforcement, most people are known by their rap sheet. Steve didn't have one until Steinhatchee, but after that, the law kept an eye on him. Once he became a fugitive, he was looked for throughout the country, and sightings of his comings and goings were rife with rumor. They thought they saw him in Miami, or Seattle and then again, he'd been spotted in Juarez. Then someone saw him in Canada. He seemed to be every place and no place. We watched his mother's funeral to see if he would show up. If he did, he was well disguised.

Granted there were more important criminals to follow—murderers, bank robbers and child molesters—but none seemed more colorful than Stephen Garrett Lamb. The thing about Steve was he was so well liked, as were many of the pot-smuggling boys of the beach, that getting anyone to provide information about his whereabouts met a dead end. Law enforcement, myself included, hate it when someone operates right under our noses and we can't catch them.

Steve followed his own drummer, worked outside the law, made his millions, was caught, served time, smuggled some more, made some more millions, got caught, served time, etc., etc., etc. You wonder what kind of businessman he might have become if he'd stayed on what I consider the Good Side.

Now he seems to be a changed man. I've known him well the past five or six years. I've watched him deal with his addictions, his lack of money, and his new life as a writer. I must admit I learned a lot from this first book of his, information I wish I'd known back then. If I had, Steve Lamb's free time might not have been so free.

Everett S. Rice, Pinellas County (Fla.) Sheriff, (ret.)

Author's Note

In 1983, years before I met Steve Lamb, my companion David tried to convince me to write a book about the drug trade in St. Petersburg during the 1960s and '70s. I told him he was nuts; no one cared. Besides that, there was too much violence connected with drugs. "But there wasn't then," he insisted. "We were just outlaws—like the Old West. Like Robin Hoods."

He persevered, telling me of his days as a marijuana dealer, buying cars for cash, bribing his teacher at Dixie Hollins High School by exchanging reefer for grades. He spoke of throwing counterfeit bills off the Skyway Bridge, of the various places drug money was buried, the friends who were caught and the ones who got away. He told of the doctors and lawyers and owners of businesses that no one would have thought were involved. He enlightened me on the consequences of heroin addiction, jumping bail and his own time in jail. And he spoke most reverentially of the adventuresome Steinhatchee Seven and the legend they'd become.

I still insisted a book on the subject was not viable. The timing wasn't right.

David died in 1995. The tale he wanted told, wasn't.

Two years ago I was hired to work on Steve's story. I was given some of his written recollections and aside from recognizing the names of some of the players, our closest connection then was that while he was busy selling funk pot at Woodstock, the festival, I was visiting art galleries in Woodstock, the village, and listening to the locals complain of the huge crowds and traffic jams.

Then I met Steve, and my first thoughts were, he's polite, he's pleasant, and—what a shame—he's burned out. How great it was to discover, over the time we put this book together, that from under all the drugging and drinking, a real talent for writing emerged. Apparently he missed his true calling.

He is the consummate insider to the early marijuana trafficking in Central Florida, a baby boomer who saw a way to turn on other boomers and at the same time, make himself rich. Although it happened in a time very different from today's blood shedding, violence-laden world of drugs, the results from what he helped unleash have been far-reaching and devastating. Steve Lamb has paid dearly for his life of smuggling and high—in every sense of the word—living. Yet if you believe, as we both do, that there are no coincidences, that everything happens for a reason, and that a merciful God has a purpose for each and every one of us, the experiences Steve shares in this book, the wise, the ridiculous, the downright dumb ass dangerous, have been a Godsend— blessings that can only be learned from and which will ultimately add to his testimony that God does perform miracles on the least of us.

(And I'd like to believe that the publishing of this story of a major marijuana entrepreneur of the beach—one of his heroes—makes David happy, too, wherever he is.)

Diane Marcou

In the Beginning

I was born November 17, 1952, in St. Petersburg, Florida, and joined the other baby boomers making their appearance all over the United States, a generation that changed the way the country was. I grew up on St. Pete Beach, a finger of an island that buffered the western edge of the city from the Gulf of Mexico. I grew up fishing and fighting, running the beaches and swimming the passes.

Sounds like a charmed life, doesn't it?

In some ways it was, because life on the beach was good.

It was life at home that was hard.

The father who left when I was six was a seaman who was hardly ever home. When he was, sometimes he was a great dad, taking me down to the pass and teaching me to fish and dive.

That was what I loved about him. However, he loved to drink, and he was a mean drunk, spending those drunken days ashore breaking and tearing up the small house we called home and treating my mother in the same hateful way. The only things he left me were an Irish name and a blond-haired, blue-eyed, freckle-faced complexion. And the ability to fish and dive. (Eventually, I learned how to drink, too, almost as well as he did.)

My mother, an angel from heaven as far as I was concerned, didn't deserve any of his meanness. She worked so hard every day waiting tables to support my sister, Susie, and me, leaving my Nana to look after us while she worked.

After Daddy left, Mom and Nana told me over and over I was now the "man of the house," so when I got a little older, I raised rabbits and cut lawns in hopes Mom wouldn't have to worry about how she'd pay the bills.

But life at home was still tough, so I spent less and less time there. It was on the beach that life was carefree.

St. Pete Beach was a virgin island full of vacant wooded land and unspoiled sandy beaches for my friends and me to call our own. No fences. No "Keep Out" signs. No "Private Property" borders to restrict us from roaming the turf. The word *condo* had still not entered my vocabulary.

One of my best friends, Rusty Stambaugh, lived at the end of the street and all the neighborhood kids hung out there. For me it was my home away from home. When we weren't at Rusty's, we'd be building forts—underground forts, tree forts, forts on the waterfront passes, and forts on the beach.

Or riding Rusty's Shetland pony, Ginger, up and down the streets of our neighborhood.

Then one day, Mom was hospitalized for a thyroid operation.

"What's gonna happen to us, Stevie?" Susie asked. "Is Mom gonna die?"

"I dunno." I didn't want to think of that, but it was hard not to. "They'll probably send us to an orphanage."

"An orphanage! No! I don't want to go to an orphanage. Couldn't we stay with Nana?"

"Nana doesn't have a job and she's really old. In fact, Mom told me she might have to start taking care of Nana soon."

"Then what about Mrs. Stambaugh? Would she take us?"

I would love to live with them! I pictured us there with all the other Stambaughs. "Naw. They've got too many kids already. They wouldn't want us, too." Then the fear came over me again. I didn't want to live with anybody else. Nana was too old to take us. Most of all, though, I didn't want Mom to die.

"What about Doris, then?" Susie broke into my thoughts. "She's Mom's best friend. We'd be with Charlie and Lisa all the time."

Doris lived just a block away. "Yeah! But she'd take you. Not me. She wouldn't want me there. Charlie and me would get in too much trouble."

"Maybe Kay and Bill would take you. They let us stay when Daddy hit Mom."

The more Sue talked, the more the thought of an orphanage seemed possible and scared the shit out of me. Having no Mom. Being alone. No ocean, no beach and no friends. As things turned out, though, Mom didn't die. She came home. The family stayed together. I didn't end up in an orphanage.

For the first time I realized that the worst fear of my life was being separated from those I loved.

Steve Lamb

ONE

"YOU KNOW WE can't afford a surfboard, Stevie. Money doesn't grow on trees."

"But I want one, Mom. I can use it instead of a boat."

"Very seldom are there waves around here for surfing. You wouldn't use it enough to justify spending the money." She turned back to the stove to stir the gravy.

"But I need it for—"

"We're not talking about this any more, you hear?"

THAT WAS THE way it always was. Not enough money. Mom crying as she counted her tips, trying to match them to the bills.

There never was enough. I couldn't stand being poor.

LATER, MOM MARRIED again. This time to Dino, a mechanic, who gave Susie and me a new little sister. When Chris was born, Sue and I were excited, and raced home from Gulf Beaches Elementary. We were so proud. I hoped now things might change; Dino drank too, just like my own father.

BY THE TIME I was twelve, my dream to have a surfboard like my friends became even stronger. In the meantime, if I wanted to go surfing with them at Sunset Beach I could only swim alongside as they paddled their boards.

Oh, how much I wanted a board. I'd make my way from St. Pete Beach to Sunset Beach, then up and down Blind Pass and out into the Gulf and on to the beaches. I'd use my board like a boat, fishing from it at spots I couldn't reach from the seawall.

Once Mom heard of me floating out Blind Pass on a strong outgoing tide, riding a wooden door taken off the back porch, she became convinced nothing would stop me.

My dream board came true on my thirteenth birthday.

A 10'3" Malibu, weighing 65 pounds. I weighed 95.

Finally Stevie Lamb had something he wanted.

I practiced as often as I could. But I had to work, too. Mom waitressed, I bussed. All tips were hers.

Working was torture to a teenager with a brand new board. From the Crow's Nest on the roof of the Holiday Inn, I watched friends playing on the beach and surfing the crystal clear waters.

We worked at the Island Club, too, where my friends' families were members. We weren't, of course. Members only were allowed to swim in the Olympic-size pool, with three diving boards (two lower and one high-dive) and attend the parties. I always had to wait outside and swim in the Gulf. Except when George Simons, the lifeguard, was busy and I sneaked in.

"Lamb, OUT! You're not members!"

Back to the saltwater, or down the beach, pool hopping.

I was determined to someday be rich.

I GOT BETTER and better at surfing, and eventually became a "hot-dogger," a surfer who does tricks or moves a board with style. It wasn't too hard nose-riding a 10'3" surfboard when I wasn't even a hundred pounds.

Along with the surfing came the girls and, of course, one hell of a sunburn. For a young teenager, I was more than eager to have a chance with the girls. On the other hand, it was the discovery of the financial benefits of marijuana that opened my eyes to a way for me and my family to live an easier life.

As I traveled to contests and surfed both coasts of Florida as much as possible, I met older surfers, saw a lot of marijuana and heard talk about its mind-altering abilities. I learned that the brown-stained fingers on most of the hottest Californians were a result of smoking

joints down to their fingertips. Most everyone's fingertips were brown except for mine. But to smoke pot, you have to buy it. Realizing how many brown fingers there were, it was the profit made from selling marijuana that intrigued me, since life at home wasn't any different—

"*You no-good sonofabitch!*" *Dino yelled as he took a swat at me.* "*Can't you never do nothin' 'round here?*"

"*Me do nothing? Look at—*" *I ducked and ran toward the door before he could smack me again.*

"*Your mother's working her ass off,*" *he called after me,* "*so you can run the beaches with your rich friends. You and that fuckin' board of yours. You're a piece of shit!*"

"*Fuck you!*" *I said, but not loud enough for him to hear. I might have been mad as hell, but I wasn't stupid.*

It was like my own dad had never left. With Dino there constantly beating my ass, and Mom struggling as hard as ever, seemed nothing had ever changed.

Marijuana—that magical money maker—was never far from my mind.

One weekend two older surfers invited me to a party in Weeki Wachee, a rural town about an hour north of St. Pete Beach.

"Everyone's gonna have reefer," Big John said. "And I mean, *everyone*. So we gotta take a matchbox with us."

"A matchbox?"

"Yeah, kid, a matchbox."

"Oh, yeah, a matchbox. Sure."

He looked at me and started laughing. "Don't tell me you don't know what a matchbox is."

Well, I didn't. But I soon learned.

Before we headed out of town, we stopped at a neighbor's and bought an actual, small, matchbox filled with marijuana, for five dollars. Five fucking dollars Red got! Just like that!

In that moment, I saw the light. My life was going to be changed forever. No more "Hey, Sonny, get over here and give me some more water." Or "Boy, go clean up that table!"

No more going home with a handful of change from busting my ass 'til late hours of the night and filling water glasses for old people who barked at me like a yard dog.

When we arrived at the ranch in Weeki Wachee, I immediately noticed I was the youngest one there, but nobody seemed to mind, so I didn't either.

Reefer and barbecue filled the air. And there I was, a part of it: I finally smoked my first joint.

I didn't feel much at first, but then as I became more aware of the people around me, the noises, and the smells, I also didn't care about the people around me, the noises and the smells. I didn't care what anyone was doing. Or saying. I was just there, enjoying the food, and *boy!* did the food taste good! Better than I'd ever tasted. Any *where*. Any *time*. Damn, that was good food! And for some reason, everything seemed funny. Didn't matter what it was, I laughed. But food and laughter aside, it was those fists-full of cash being exchanged for a little plant that remained uppermost in my mind.

I knew I had to get a piece of that action.

After that trip, as I busted my back cutting lawns, butchering rabbits, and still bussing tables for change, I kept thinking of all the people I knew who smoked pot. If I could just get my hands on some to sell, I knew I could make big money. And I knew the perfect place to do it. The Corner Pocket Pool Hall, my main hangout, two blocks from home.

The Corner Pocket was a prime marketplace for gambling on any kind of bet. It offered a hungry kid like me a first-class education in street smarts. To get my foot in the door, I told Charlie I'd help him around the place. I checked out balls, swept tables, and cleaned up. After working there a while, Denny, an older, well-known pool hustler I'd known most of my life, came up to me.

"Hey, Steve. How you doing?" he asked.

"Getting by, I guess. Nothing to brag about but holding my own."

"Been surfing much?"

"Much as I can."

"Hard to make any money surfin', ain't it?"

"Yeah, but it's fun. And great exercise. And girls love surfers."

"Well, I've got a proposition. You could make some money, I could make some money . . . know what I mean?"

I nodded. I didn't know what the hell he was talking about, for sure, but figured it was something a little shady.

"Look here," he said. "You got friends smoking pot?"
I nodded.

"Thought you did. Who doesn't?" He laughed. "You smoke a little, too?"

"Maybe. Now and then." I didn't want to sound like I wasn't cool.

"You know, I was thinking you might be just the person I'm looking for. How 'bout me giving you some reefer to sell for me. Think you could do that?"

Could I do that? Joy ran through my veins. How could I turn him down? He was a good-hearted man who knew how to make money in all kinds of ways—just the kind of guy I needed.

I was in business. The light was green.

When he offered to front me ten lids for a hundred dollars—ten Glad sandwich bags filled to the max—I was really surprised. I didn't know there was that much marijuana so close by. I sold them for fifteen dollars each. I made fifty dollars! That was more money than my mother could make in tips in a week waiting tables. And even though I made money off of them, the friends I sold the lids to praised me for the deal. It was hugs, handshakes, and everyone was happy.

I liked spreading that love and joy that came with reefer! That was nice, but I felt better being paid for it. It was definitely a blessing. With demand high and supply low, I figured there was no limit to the profits I could make. Then Wilson Hubbard offered me a summer job and with working on his party boats, I had even more money.

AS I SHOWED my ability to move marijuana in a fast and trusted way, it became a supplemental income for my family. But my new found wealth was kind of obvious.

"What? You've got *more* money for me?" Mom eyed me with a questioning look. "You can't be making that much in tips on Hubbard's boats. Where's all this extra cash coming from?"

"Shootin' pool, Mom," I lied. "Charlie's teaching me everything he knows. I'm getting better and better."

"Well, isn't he nice, looking out for you that way," she said, satisfied her son was under the guidance of such a caring friend. She had no reason to suspect otherwise, and besides, she was pleased by my help with the bills.

As fast as I received the lids, the faster they were gone. But I needed more weight to even consider making serious money. Getting a handful of lids once or twice a week was great money compared to what my family and I were used to, but now that I had a taste of what it was like to make such easy cash, I was determined to go for the gold.

My goals were set for millions. And through it all I'd spread joy, happiness and brotherly love providing God's herb to the people. Was there any better way to make a million?

I didn't care that there were no large quantities of marijuana coming in at this time. I knew that no matter how long or what it took, I was not going to let anything stop me.

I SPENT LOTS of time fishing with Mike Knight, a hard working friend I'd known all my life. He was so connected to the water I sometimes thought he was part fish. He loved the water as much as I did. In fact, he loved everything about the water—the fish, the salt, the surf. I watched him over and over again unloading thousands of pounds of mullet off the boat he'd built.

"Hey, Mike. You ever need a hand?"

"Why, Bo Weevil? You fixin' to be a mullet fisherman?"

We went to different schools during the day, then fished together late afternoons and nights, many times into the early morning hours. Then we'd worry about getting to school on time. In the fall of the year, mullet traveled by the millions, like interstates of fish. If a pelican swooped low over a large school of them, the fish would shower the water for a quarter mile. On those days, we were sometimes late for school.

But most times we'd manage to make it from schools of fish to schools of classes, though often, smelling like a fish house.

The more we fished, the more we learned about the moon and its effect on the tides and the fish. Eventually we could navigate the flats, the potholes, and the mangrove islands on both sides of the Tampa Bay estuary with our eyes closed.

As I went through junior high I surfed and fished, but mostly stayed on top of my lid business, buying a pound or two when available. It was a good thing, because now, more than ever, my mother needed me.

She'd been diagnosed with lung cancer and we thought we were going to lose her. Before she went into surgery, she hung onto my arm. "Stevie, promise me you'll get your high school diploma. I'm so afraid of not being there to keep you in school."

"I give you my word, Mom, I'll get my diploma." I kissed her and prayed she'd not die.

She didn't, but she went through chemotherapy and radiation, her back burned so badly Sue and I had to keep it covered with a moisturizing cream several times a day. She was out of work quite a while and the family income suffered. For that reason, I knew I had to find a bigger and better connection to marijuana. I could sell much more than I was receiving. I had to support my family.

I fished and hung out at Hubbard's Pier on Eighth Avenue on Pass-A-Grille. If I wasn't at the pool hall, I was at the Pier or at Pass-A-Grille Beach. It was the main meeting place for sometimes as many as hundreds of kids who lived on or near there.

Many of my older friends were being drafted for service in Vietnam and I knew my time was not far off. Anti-war movements, freedom movements and the widespread use of drugs sprang up. Much of the country's younger population joined the hippie movement and its message of love, peace, and flower power.

I was all for love and peace. But it wasn't flower power I had in mind; pot power was in my sights.

And it was a grand time to sell marijuana.

There was a need for grass from coast to coast. As the war continued, many men sent to fight were introduced to grass, opium and heroin overseas. As soldiers were sent back to the U.S., drugs came with them. There was a lot of drug smuggling from Vietnam to the United States. Most of it was a white powder, China white. Heroin. But with this smuggling of heroin came some of the best pot in the world from Vietnam.

A few guys came to me and offered me some Thai stick deals. I was overwhelmed by their offers. Up until then, all I'd ever known was Mexican pot. Thai sticks were a whole other ball game.

Much of it was soaked in opium. The pot I was receiving was some of the best smoke in the world. When Thai came from Vietnam, it usually came in less than a pound. Business was good. People would pay anything. It was a status symbol just to own Thai sticks and most of it was bought to smoke, not to sell.

Because of my connections with the Thai sticks, I now had the guys I'd been selling for, buying from me. The only problem for me was same old story: there was never enough of it.

TWO

AS I STARTED high school it seemed every one I knew was getting into drugs, one kind or another. Fraternity parties were once weekend alcohol binges, where to be a man meant you were so drunk you vomited everything in your system or passed out and needed some friend to drop you off in your front yard beat up or half naked. These now became fraternity cookouts where everyone had big bags of smoke. Behavior changed at the school keg parties, beach parties at Tierra Verde, and rock concerts at the National Guard Armory. People had a tendency to fight when drinking. With marijuana use, all of us just sat on the beaches and seawalls, enjoyed the music and each other, united in harmony. It seemed the times of fistfights and useless drunken brawls were coming to an end.

Everyone, it seemed, was on drugs and not just the illegal ones.

Mother's little helpers; speed to make it through a hard day's work; diet pills to keep the weight off; Codeine for your cough; Percodans for the backache; Quaaludes for stress and headaches; Seconals, Nembutals, Tuinals, Valiums to relax or put you to sleep; Black Beauties to wake you up. Many bathroom medicine cabinets had more drugs and stronger drugs than you would find in a pain management clinic today.

The first of each month I raced my sister to Mom's or Nana's medicine cabinet for their Quaaludes. Mom received sixty 714s every month, and my grandmother, sixty 712s, 150 milligrams of methaquaalude, half the size of a 714. They were candy for us kids. Everyone loved them. And wow! How they helped us score. Cupid definitely worked on us with those pills. No one could do wrong when on 714s, except kill themselves and everyone around them if they were driving an automobile.

"Oh, I can drive," they'd say. Sure; everyone knew how to drive while high on Quaaludes. Right into a wall, a tree, or another car.

There were many fatal automobile accidents caused by people high on Quaaludes and eventually the government outlawed the drug. At the time, it was one of the most prescribed drugs there was.

So please, let's not blame this drug problem on marijuana because 'it's illegal.'

The fact is, I thought that we, as a people, would be doing much better if pot were legal. And that I truly believed. If I was going to make a living selling something, I had to believe in it. Selling peace, joy and God's-grown love in a bag would do you much better than a bottle of whiskey. I didn't see anything good written about a bottle of whiskey in the Bible, but I often told people to check out Genesis, the first book of the Bible, Chapter 1, verses 11-12.

I enjoyed smoking reefer and it never made me want to fight, or drive crazy, and not once did I end up with a hangover. Marijuana just made me happy, horny and hungry.

But I did get into drugs for the money.

Back at Boca Ciega High School, I had no plans of becoming a career criminal. It just seemed to happen.

The time and place were the breeding grounds for many a fine smuggler.

I never really was much for school, preferring fishing when I should have been schooling. I couldn't get my mind into the books when I knew it was high tide and the water was crystal clear and there were schools of snook, trout, redfish and mullet with my name on them.

But I also knew school was the right thing to do and I didn't want to be a high school dropout. I was going to get my diploma so I did my best being a schoolboy: fraternity, wrestling team, track team and an average student. It just happened that opportunities came up that were unrelated to school.

I was doing very well during my sophomore year, moving small quantities of weed, and I had a lot of contacts now.

As it turned out, the opportunity that didn't include school put a damper on my high school education. That opportunity included traveling, and making more money in one trip than my teacher could make in six months. Plus surfing some of the best waves in the world.

The deal was offered to me by two older friends, Jim and Charlie, who had moved to San Diego to surf and buy cheaper marijuana. They needed two guys to mule kilos of Mexican marijuana from San Diego to Hilo on the main island. What a dream come true. And the money I'd be making was unheard of.

Buying Mexican pot on the Mexican border or in Tijuana was much cheaper and there was weight available.

They said they'd pay for the tickets for me and Albert, a guy I'd surfed and grown up with, if we wanted to come out there. Who could turn down an offer like that?

They had a beautiful house in Sunset Cliffs in San Diego County overlooking the Pacific Ocean, with some of the most beautiful waves I had ever set eyes on breaking right out their back yard.

The house was set a few hundred feet above the ocean, and you could look out the back deck and see the Coronado Islands. There was also a breathtaking view of miles and miles of Mexican and Californian coastline.

It was the first time I had ever set eyes on the Pacific. The coastline was nothing like Florida. There were crystal clear waves to the west and snow-capped peaks back to the east. There was a beauty like I'd never seen before.

My San Diego friends bought marijuana for $35 to $70 a kilo, depending on the quality and where it was bought. We flew them to Hilo and sold them for $250 a block. Albert and I were paid $30 a block for each unit we transported and we usually carried forty keys a trip, averaging $1,200 each time, plus expenses. I flew one week, Albert the next.

We worked with a Hawaiian Japanese syndicate, big Hawaiian mokes who looked like OddJob, the big Japanese guy in the James Bond film, *Goldfinger,* who threw his hat at the statue and cut off its head.

They'd pick us up at the airport in an old gangster-looking, Bonnie-and-Clyde type car and take us to a big two-story house right on the Pacific Ocean. We were always treated like royalty and never had a problem with money. Business with these guys was sweet. They took good care of us and loved showing us around their islands.

When I wasn't in Hawaii, I was in a beautiful house in San Diego partying and loving life. Everything was new and exciting. Life was a joy and full of new adventures. We started flying to other islands, Oahu and Maui and made some very good Hawaiian friends. One even moved to St. Petersburg and continued being a close friend.

We muled for several months. When I left Florida, I was a *hundred*aire. I traveled, partied, surfed, went diving and marlin fishing, and experienced an adventure of a lifetime. When I returned, my financial situation was much different. I came back with more memories than I had ever dreamed of. I also came back a *thousand*aire, with about fifteen thousand dollars.

I helped my mother out, got my own apartment and bought an Econoline van, my first set of wheels, for $400. I had it going on. I was 16 years old.

But what really put me in the ball game were the two Samsonite suitcases I'd brought home to St. Pete Beach. They were filled with about forty keys.

They ended up at my old friend's house, the one who used to front me the lids that I would sell for him. Now things had changed.

I was the one with the unbelievable weight and at an unbelievable price. I was the one now selling reefer to Big Denny. I fronted the blocks to him for $250 a block, and he was in hog heaven. It was all handshakes and hugs.

DENNY AND I were definitely involved in the reefer business now. He had a contact in Tampa where he told me he was going to buy fifty pounds at $150 a pound. Would I be interested in investing? I sure would.

We went over to Tampa and turned onto Bayshore Boulevard and drove to a nice house on the water where we were to make the transaction.

We had $7,500 in hundreds for the reefer, and $600 in ghetto money—ones, fives and tens—pure pocket paper—to pay the person who owned the house. We sat in a waterfront living room with the owner for close to an hour past the time we were supposed to receive the product. It was then there was a loud explosion. Denny and I came two feet off the couch.

"What the hell was that?" Denny yelled.

"Sounded like a gunshot."

I thought it smelled like one, too. We started searching the house to see where the noise came from. I went through the kitchen door into the darkened garage. I saw an open door to what I assumed was a bathroom. Seeing a pair of tennis shoes, I jumped back into Denny who was right behind me.

"Whoa, there," he said. "Someone in there?"

"I thought it was, but it's just a pair of white tennis shoes. It's so dark I thought it was somebody. But don't you smell the gunpowder?"

I walked back in to check the smell and immediately was jabbed in the chest with a shotgun.

"Get in the living room, motherfucker," some guy yelled, pushing me in that direction. "You too, fat boy. Get your fat ass in there."

The owner of the house came running into the kitchen and was quickly herded up with us.

"On your stomachs! Keep your face down! Hey you, big boy. Take your pants off. Then take this tape and tie your buddies up."

Denny removed his pants and standing in his underwear, taped my hands behind my back. As I looked up to get a look at the gunman, he kicked me square in the face. "Motherfucker! Keep your face buried in that carpet or I'll blow your head off."

I sneaked a look anyway and saw him, holding the gun in the crook of his arm, tie Denny's arms behind his back. "Now get on the floor, motherfucker!"

He paced back and forth, cursing, kicking us in the head as he went. Thank God he had tennis shoes on.

"Where's the damn money?" He started patting me down. All I had on was a pair of corduroy shorts. He then checked Denny's pants on the floor, and pulled out a three or four inch stack of money.

"That's more like it."

He went into the kitchen and started tearing up the drawers. I could hear him bagging up the silverware. A few minutes later he came back, and started kicking us again. "I'm gonna blow your fuckin' heads off!" he hollered. I was scared to death.

I could see he still had hold of the shotgun. I tried to get a look at him and caught a shoe in the ear.

"Motherfucker, you wanna look at somethin'? I'm gonna show you your balls!"

He pulled a butter knife out of the bag and tried to cut my shorts off, holding me up off the floor. I was so fuckin' scared I thought I was going to shit myself.

"You skinny little sonofabitch! I'm gonna cut your balls off and stick 'em in your mouth! I told you to keep your fuckin' face down." He picked up Denny's pants again.

"Fat boy," he snarled, "I'm takin' your keys and your car!" He grabbed Denny's keys from his pants pocket, then began messing with me, kicking and holding me up off the floor, trying to cut off my shorts again.

"You bony little bastard! I'm gonna cut your balls off!"

When was he gonna start fuckin' with the *owner* of the house and leave me alone?

KaBOOM! Both barrels of the shotgun rang again, this time right next to me. He dropped me back to the floor. Parts of the ceiling fell on us and we were covered with dust and plaster.

"Keep your faces to the floor, motherfuckers. I'm goin' out the front and I have a friend across the street with a rifle. Anyone come out that door and you're dead. Stay right here on the floor. You move, you're dead."

The front door slammed.

"That dumb sonofabitch shoulda had one of you guys tie me up," Denny said. "Holdin' on to that shotgun, he only used one hand to tie me." Denny snapped his lightly wrapped wrists and grabbed the knife. In a moment he'd cut both of us free.

"Hey, you got any guns in this house?" I asked the owner, "I need one now!" I followed him to the master bedroom where he handed me a small pistol, a .32. Denny darted to a gun rack and pulled off a long Davy Crockett-type gun.

I ran out the front door and saw that the guy was having a hard time getting Denny's fastback Mustang into reverse. By the time he did, and backed out into the street, I was twenty feet away from the car. I emptied the pistol, a few bullets into the passenger door and one of them into a rear tire, blowing it out.

Big 350-pound Denny was right behind me in his little Fruit of the Loom underwear. He jumped on a bike he grabbed from someone who happened to be passing by, and went after the gunman.

So there was the Mustang, screeching, scraping and flying sparks down the street, almost-naked Denny on the bicycle pedaling after the car holding onto his Davy Crockett gun, and me, covered with plaster dust and swinging my empty pistol—but still with my balls—running after Denny.

It seemed as if the whole neighborhood was out in their front yards watching the road race.

We came upon the car parked on a dead end vacant lot. The cops and the neighbors were right behind us, only to find an empty car full of bloody bandages. This must not have been the first time he'd encountered someone who didn't like him. The gunman had jumped into a creek, swum over to some mangroves and made his escape.

We were questioned by the police. One officer, noting Denny's gun, asked, "Just what did you intend to do with that?"

"Shoot the crazy bastard!"

"With what? You got fake gunpowder for your fake muzzleloader? This gun don't do nothin' but look nice on a wall."

The police called a taxi and a tow truck, and said the car would be towed to a pound to be used as evidence. Denny went to get in the car.

The officer stopped him. "Nope. Can't let you."

"I've got my money in the back."

"I thought he got the money, Denny," I said.

"Oh, yeah. That's right. He did. But not all of it."

The officer then questioned us about the money. Denny told him we were waiting to buy a race boat at a house on the water and got set up. That satisfied the police and we were able to get back to St. Pete.

That was one helluva day.

A week later, in my sister's boyfriend's old yellow Volkswagen, I went to pick up some pot in another deal. After what had happened, since I was once again dealing with a friend of a friend, I decided for the first time to carry a gun. I wanted to keep my balls if something went wrong.

With the guy who knew where the pot was as my passenger, I drove the Volkswagen to a ranch someplace outside of Seminole, then down a little dirt road that ended at a fence. "Okay, we'll wait here," the guy said.

I stopped, rolled down the window and settled down to wait. "I don't ever carry a gun," I explained, "but you know, I got robbed last week by some crazy bastard who was gonna cut my balls off, so this time, to keep us safe, I brought a gun—"

Click. "That's exactly what *this* is," I heard in my left ear.

Another fucking setup.

They took the money, the gun and Pat's car. I walked and hitchhiked all night, getting home at daybreak.

"Hey, Pat. I—"

23

"Where the hell you *been?* My dad'll kill me. I've been waitin' here with Susie all night. You said you'd be gone for an hour. Where have you been? Where's my car?"

"I lost it."

"You what? You lost my car? How the hell—"

"I got robbed, Pat. We'll go look for it. It's got to be somewhere in Seminole. Out by those lakes."

About one o'clock that afternoon, on a dirt road, there was Pat's little yellow canary. At least he had his car back. I'd lost my money, again. I'd lost my friend's gun. I decided I was done fucking with people around here who "knew" people who wanted to sell. From now on, I thought, I'm sticking with people *I* know.

I figured I might have to go to California, but at least I wouldn't get ripped off. I'd done business out there before, and knew where to get the best prices as well as any weight I wanted. I truly had a moneymaking ability at hand.

But before I started running coast to coast like a wild man, I was going to Cocoa Beach to rent a trailer at Oceanic Trailer Park, see some old friends, and do some surfing.

I was king of the road driving across Florida to Cocoa on I-4 in the Econoline van. As I was headed east getting closer to Cocoa Beach, I picked up a long-haired hippie type, a wiry little fellow who was thumbing a ride.

"Where you headed?"

"Cocoa," he answered, climbing in the van.

"You're in luck. That's right where I'm going."

"Hey, man, far out!" he said, looking stoked. "I'm hitching across the country. Started out in California."

He was a dusty little Clint Eastwood-type dude but appeared to be truthful and honest, a real road dog and one hell of a nice guy. He was a little short on money.

I had some.

He was a little short on soap.

I had some.

Short on food.

I gave him some.

What he didn't seem to know, was he was just plain short. He was such a little fellow.

Further down the road, after listening to him begin every sentence, "Hey, man, there are fields and fields of herb all throughout the mid states of our country;" "Hey, man, I'm telling you the truth;" "Hey, man, it's for real;" I nicknamed him 'Hey Man Dave.'

Hey Man Dave told me of fields of marijuana in Iowa, Nebraska, and Kansas. He said the government planted it in World War II, making hemp rope for parachutes out of the stalks.

This was a hard one for me to believe. States filled with great fields of reefer in our country, the U.S. of A?

I decided to check out his story.

A few weeks later, Albert, his friend, Larry, and I drove to Sioux City, Iowa in Larry's GTO. We took hedge clippers and branch trimmers. And boxes and boxes of garbage bags. I really didn't know how we would find it or what even to look for, but as it turned out, just like Hey Man Dave said, it was all over the roadsides and riverbanks. Marijuana as far as you could see.

Larry dropped Albert and me at the edge of a riverbank next to a bridge.

"Come back here at five," I told him. "That'll give us most of the day."

Larry drove off and we looked around.

"Gotta be the armpit of the world," Albert said. "Lookit here; no one for miles."

"Yeah, and nothing but open fields of crops and hemp."

Excited by what was ahead of us, we gathered our clippers, bags, water and other supplies.

"Let's head for that tree," I said, pointing to a big tree in the middle of the field. "We can unload this stuff there."

We slipped through a fence into a field of hemp, an overgrowth taller than we stood that was so thick we could have gotten lost walking side by side.

We unloaded our supplies at the tree, gathered our clippers and trimmers, and began attacking twelve-foot high plants that had stalks like little trees. Clippers were useless on many on them.

We were blessed. We were in overhead plants, as many solid buds as we could cut. More females than we would want to cut in a lifetime. The plants were so big and thick our clippers would not cut through some of them. We cut just the tops and the long bud branches, collecting mounds of them and filling our four-foot garbage bags. It was backbreaking work.

We had a lot to learn.

For one thing, aside from the hard work involved, we had to be sure that we carried everything out, leaving nothing behind. For another, we knew we had to watch for a pit bull since we'd been warned many farmers kept them as guard dogs. But this farmer had his own *bull*— and it wasn't a dog—to keep peace in his field.

Every time we entered or left that day, we had to worry about being run down by a thousand-pound beef master.

The weeds and brush and the big tree in the middle of the field saved us a couple of times, and I felt like a running back, only carrying bales of reefer and supplies instead of a football. What a running game.

A few times we had to slip the fence short of the bridge due to that thousand-pound nightmare right behind us. Instead of being at the bridge we had to walk the muddy riverbank.

"Ain't you worried 'bout leaving footprints?" Albert asked.

"Who'd know? It's not like we're gonna be sticking around."

We made it to the bridge and waited underneath for Larry. Eventually we heard a motor, but it was no GTO. It was going too slow.

And I mean *s-l-o-w.*

Albert looked worried. "That's not Larry."

I peeked up over the bridge. "Damn, it's not. It's a tractor. Can't be going more than a couple miles an hour." I sat back down and waited.

When the tractor finally hit the bridge, we listened to its heavy weight as it slowly made its way. When it was directly over our heads, it stopped. There was no sound other than the motor.

"You think he's gonna look under here?" Albert whispered.

"Why'd he do that?"

"Dunno; but he could."

I wasn't as calm as I pretended, but I knew it would do no good to get nervous. If he did find us under here we'd have to think fast. But he left after about five very long minutes and crawled away from us. If he suspected anything, it'd be a while before he'd be able to reach anyone at the speed he was going. Ten minutes later we heard the welcome sounds of Larry in his GTO.

We hurriedly loaded the trunk with the bales of our buds and jumped in the car.

"Haul ass," I told Larry.

He headed down a dirt road from nowhere, and as we rode the twelve to fifteen miles back to the paved road, Albert and I boasted of our job well done.

Just as we hit the main paved road and headed toward the Interstate and our room at the Holiday Inn, Larry glanced in his rear view mirror and laughed.

"Look behind us," he yelled.

I turned around. Two Iowa State Troopers' cars stormed down the dirt road we'd turned off shortly before.

Once at the Holiday Inn, we backed the car up to the door of our ground floor room and unloaded the bales. Stems and branches poked out of the plastic bags, making them look like we were lugging giant porcupines. We had to clean the buds off many of the branches. Many of the branches? The whole load was branches of buds. And as it was, the pot began to sweat.

"We've got to air this out," I told the guys. "We've got to strip all these buds from the stems."

So we stripped and stripped, branch after branch. And then stripped some more branches. The three of us sat up all night stripping the buds, twice as much work as the cutting had been.

We filled the bathtub four to five feet high with three-foot stems that were once branches filled with buds. When we finally finished, it seemed like half the bathroom was filled with stems and the floor covered with buds on plastic garbage bags.

"Hit the A/C," I told Albert. "There's not much time. We've got to dry these buds out."

He cranked the air conditioner way down and cold air blasted into the room.

Larry looked at the mess of bare stems that filled the bathroom. "And what are we going to do with these?"

"Leave 'em," Albert said.

Larry scowled. "You crazy? The room's in our names."

"Here, grab these," I said, pulling off all the bed sheets and spreading them on the floor. "Let's fill 'em."

We filled the sheets with the stems and tied them off, then thanking God for hanging ceilings that have removable squares, lifted out a few squares and crammed the bed sheets-made bales into the roof overhead.

"That'll be a surprise for someone some day," Larry said, replacing the last square back into the ceiling.

The next morning we cleaned up the room and the bathtub, put just the buds in the new garbage bags, filled the trunk and checked out. We headed southbound back to Florida, back to St. Pete Beach.

THE HARVEST FROM that Iowa field had been quite an example of marijuana growing: As the summer days had gotten shorter, the plants had gotten bigger and the buds on the females thicker and longer. The females were the only plants we'd been interested in.

By the time we hit home base and broke into the bales, the pot looked like spinach and had a funky smell to it. (For that reason and the fact it doesn't really get you high, it is still called "funk pot" today.) But it sure looked great once it was dried out and pressed into kilo-size blocks with sugar water sprayed on the buds to hold their form in a block.

To make the blocks, I had a press made: Two three-foot sheets of quarter-inch steel welded at all four corners with four steel bars. There was one sheet on the bottom and the other one, two feet higher. I also had four open-top and face boxes welded into kilo size. I lined these with meat wrapping paper.

Once the pot was put into the kilo-size boxes, I had a top that slid into the box. I would put four boxes under the roof of steel, lay a pound of pot in each box, then spray the first pounds in the boxes with sugar water, and then slide in the top. Next, jack the free-fitting top of the box down with a hydraulic car jack.

I had four jacks, one for each box. That way I was able to press four blocks at a time. After the first pound of weed was under pressure for fifteen to twenty minutes, I released the jacks, slid off the tops, weighed the second pound, sprayed it with the sweet sticky stuff, put the four steel tops back into place and jacked them down again, tightly, for the required fifteen to twenty minutes.

After the second pound was formed into the first pound, I had a perfect two-pound kilo. I then released the pressure and slid out the tops.

I pulled the paper out the open face of the boxes, wrapped them just like Christmastime, taped the ends, taped the middle and there you had it: four beautiful-looking kilos.

We were doing eight keys, sixteen pounds, an hour. When we were done, we had blocks stacked up like a wall, a little over a hundred fifty pounds. Which meant fifty pounds apiece.

Which meant we each made seven or eight grand. Not bad for three kids and a week's work.

Again, I thanked God that farmer had a slow, s-l-o-w tractor.

EVERYONE KNEW OUR secret after moving that hundred fifty pounds on our little strip of St. Petersburg Beach. Once word got out of fields of marijuana in the mid states of our country, Southern beach boys were migrating northbound with vans and trunks full of clippers and bags. They were making thousands off hemp. Having smoked that funk pot myself a few times, I was surprised it sold like it did. Hell, it didn't even get you high. And the *smell*.

I did one more trip to Iowa and back in a van, but by the time I was at the beach in Florida, the place was flooded with funk pot. I even tried a few contacts I knew out of state, and they, too, were flooded. Everyone had it and people were selling pounds for almost nothing. It wasn't worth doing another trip up North, or at least not that summer. We still had almost half the van full of blocks from that second trip because we couldn't sell shit!

Beautiful blocks of buds, no one wanted.

But about a week after blocking everything up and having no luck moving it, another blessing arrived.

There was a lot of talk about a grand shindig that was going to happen in New York, in a place called Woodstock. It was said there would be a weeklong festival of music and drugs, nonstop. With the kinds of musicians who were playing, there should be a helluva group of people. Like a school of mullet in the fall.

Mammal and Chaz, neighbors of mine, and I were ready to go.

What better place to sell pot than at a pop festival with that many people. It was a two-day drive and we had a week to get there. It was *adios* to Florida.

Once again we were headed north. We wanted to leave early to get a good parking place in the parking lot. Hell, as it turned out, there was no parking lot! It took two days of idling along just to get to the edge of a grand, grand campground. For as far as your eye could see, people were camped out in tents, vans, and cars, and we were just at the edge of it.

Talk about a party. People were walking around bug-eyed, half naked, or for that matter, butt naked. Making love right in the middle of fields, tents, on cars, in big groups, dancing. Holding up signs, *Flower Power, Freedom Movement, No War.*

Herb filled the air. People had open drugstores of drugs on tables, laid out on the floors of their vans, on the hoods of cars or in their tents. People walked around yelling—some even with bullhorns—"LSD!" "Mescaline!" "Reefer!" "Hash!" "Speed!" "Uppers!" "Downers!"

Police on horseback rode right by them, not doing a thing. What could they do? There were miles and miles of crazy, tripped-out people.

We were a few days early and it was more than a mile and a half of solid people between us and the stage where they were going to be playing the music. People came in steadily, like lines of ants.

The party was on. Now was as good a time as any to break out the product. But we had to be very, very careful. Half the van was full of blocks. In fact, the whole van floor was a solid bed. We spread sleeping bags and blankets over the blocks and slept two-and-a-half feet off the floor of the van.

Chaz, at 250 pounds the biggest one of us, put on this blanket-type Mexican poncho that hung to his knees, and would take eight to ten blocks and put them under the poncho. Mammal and I walked in front of him, telling people that we had keys of marijuana for $250 apiece.

We dealt, traded and bargained with all kinds of people, who invited us into their camps, tents and vans, or just wanted to sit on the ground where we stood, get high, and talk business.

"Let's look at the block." "Hey, let's open it." "Let's try it." "Let's weigh it." "Let's play with it." Half of them were so high they couldn't even see the pot, let alone taste it. It was taking much too long to negotiate each block.

We didn't want anyone to know where the pot was, so Chaz stood back a few hundred feet, in the middle of a sea of people, his arms full of keys under his Mexican poncho blanket, and no one realized it.

The first few days, people weren't carrying much money. Most of the dealers—which was almost everyone—had their money invested in their drugs they brought to sell: pills of every size and color, hash, and a few with marijuana. The paper trail was not far behind. As each day passed, the dealers had fewer drugs to sell and more money to buy with. The first couple of days we mostly traded pot for whatever they had to trade—like LSD, mescaline, peyote, Seconals, Tuinals, and Quaaludes. In other words, every prescription drug a pharmacy had, plus a few they didn't.

What really saved us was trading one of our keys for two ounces of kick-ass hash and a pipe. Yeah. What a deal. This hash pipe turned out to be our lifesaver. It had been smoked with so much good hash a person could light the pipe with nothing in it and still get high.

Our pockets began filling with money. The sales pitch came with the pipe. "No time to sit down. No time to roll a joint, eat and shoot the shit. We have business to take care of. Here, if you're interested, tear a little hole in the paper, take a pinch. We have a pipe."

Now a pinch of our funk pot in the magical pipe.

"Be careful now. It's strong weed. A big hit and you have to cough to get off. Take a hit. If you like the taste of it, buy it. If you don't like the taste, don't buy it. Easy. We've got business to take care of. We've gotta go. We don't have time to sit down and smoke a joint with every person we meet."

They'd light it and take a hit, and the person thought they were smoking Thai sticks.

"Hey, that's good herb. Has the hashy taste. I'll buy one; no, gimme two of 'em."

"Yeah. Sure."

This made moving our product much easier and faster. Each passing day our beds in the van got closer to the floor and our stacks of green paper got bigger and bigger.

ON THE DAY the festival started and the music began, we slipped through fields and fields of people, sitting, lying down, jumping around, dancing, making love. Hell, yeah. You go, people. Go.

Nothing like being butt naked, making love in the middle of a million people, while Jimi Hendrix, Janis Joplin, Grateful Dead, Richie Havens, Mountain and many more were putting on their own performances.

We had people coming back for thirds, fourths and fifths. They were making money off it. When they found out we were out, they cried. We were happy.

We were sold out of blocks by the second day of the music.

So the rest of the week was—*wow!* you just had to be there to understand. An experience one could never explain in a million words. Beauty and fear. Hundreds of thousands of people going hog-wild. OD tents set up throughout the grounds for the ones who were space bound or took too much of whatever they took. Tripping in the middle of a million people with Hendrix eating his guitar right in front of you. We could have sold a ton of blocks. The higher people got, the faster the blocks went. It was a week of nonstop boogie. Drugs, music, and a lot of loving. Not a bad combo. This was a one-week nonstop flight. What a trip it was. Yeah. What a great time. And we all got paid for it.

We headed back south with thirty thousand dollars, each one of us a *ten thousand*aire, and we also had our gallon jug of every drug in the world, every buzz known to man.

Back home I felt like I had all the money in the world. And my sister definitely had it rocking with all the pills she was stealing from my cookie jar that I'd brought back from New York. I gave Mom a stack of money to pay a few months' bills and to buy a new refrigerator. I figured she'd be colder than the freezer on the fridge wondering where the money came from, but this time, she didn't ask.

Summer was coming to an end and fall wasn't far behind. It was time for school. My extended vacation from Boca Ciega last year while I muled back and forth from Hawaii, kept me from going back to Bogie. School now had to be Tomlinson Adult Education at Mirror Lake where I promised to fulfill Mom's dream of my getting a high school diploma. A GED would have to do. She would be happy with that. I enrolled and had every intention of getting that GED. A few months later, something else came along and I fucked up again.

Albert, my surfing buddy, wanted us to go to Eleuthera, the eastern most island in the Bahamian chain, to a spot named Surfer's Beach. Some of the biggest and best waves in the Bahamas broke there.

THREE

MOM WASN'T HAPPY with my new idea. "You can't go surfing," she said. "You need to get your diploma. You need to stay in school. Remember, you promised me!" So I gave her my word I'd get one.

I talked to a good friend, Billy, a very smart guy, a straight-A student, who had just finished high school. I wanted to hire him to go to a north county school and enroll in my name. "Just go. No one will know you're not Stevie Lamb."

He came up with a better idea. He said for three pounds a month or two ounces of that kick-ass hash, he would enroll at a high school with an adult education course. "I'll have you your GED," Bill told me. "It'll be all nice and legal-like in your name."

"Sounds great. That'll take care of my promise to Mom. In the meantime, I'll surf and make you money, while you're doing my schooling for me."

So I was off to Eleuthera and Bill was off to school. This kind of schooling I could handle with a smile.

Albert and I surfed Eleuthera for a week and caught some very big waves. We fished in Hatchett Bay, where a chicken processing plant let blood and guts run into the bay. It was shark heaven, a fun place to fish, but we did our diving on the other side of the island.

The waves were so good in Eleuthera and the trip was such an experience, I decided to take another one. After all, Bill was still going to school for me; I could do what I wanted.

A friend, Greg LaForge, was living in Barbados, West Indies, and like Eleuthera in the Bahamas, Barbados was the eastern most island in the West Indies, and caught all the best swells in the Atlantic. Seeing it was now fall, it had access to the big northerly swells coming in out of the North.

The island was so neat and beautiful. I was having such a good time surfing, fishing, and diving, and just cruising around in a golf cart-type little car they called a Moke, driving on the left side of the road, just the opposite of the States. I had a blast driving around the island, going up the snake-shaped roads into the beautiful tropical mountains and beeping the horn before every curve, then going down the snaky mountain roads to the sea. It was like driving on a go-cart course all the time. The place was so beautiful I constantly thought about my mother. She always said her dream was to go to an island before she died. I longed for her to be beside me. I was definitely going to send Mom to the islands of her dreams before she did die. I owed that to her.

Greg and I lived on the south coast in a little boat-builders' town where all the natives built their boats by hand and out of wood—no fiberglass. We lived right on the beach in a small wooden house. It was a treat talking with the natives about fishing and the kind of fish they caught and watching them build their boats. The craftsmanship and boat-building abilities they had were unbelievable.

We surfed clean, crystal clear little perfect waves on the south coast of the island. You could see the fish in the reef right through the face of the waves, that were top to bottom barrels. With the lip of the wave throwing over your back, you'd enter into a crystal clear hole of ecstasy and joy. The water was so clear it seemed as though you were flying on your surfboard. But the big double, triple, overhead mountains of water came in on the North and Northeast coast. At a little town called Bathsheba, a houseful of Americans lived.

Bathsheba was a surfer's hangout, filled with American and local surfers. We surfed all day, then took freshwater showers and had giant cookouts on the beach. Bathsheba was only forty-five minutes across the mountain range to the south coast where we lived, but many a time we were surfed out, and seeing the wooden house was nothing but bedrooms and a shower, we often stayed over for a few days when the swell was big. Sometimes the waves were so large you didn't know how you were going to get in once you got out.

My seventeenth birthday was, according to the locals, the biggest day in many years. The swell was so big, no one went out.

The whole north coast was closed out, so seeing it was my birthday, everyone decided to have a party for me.

We first hit the cow fields, picking the magic mushrooms, and then made the mind-altering tea. They toasted my birthday, again and again and again, and we probably drank more than we should have. As everyone started enjoying the spectrums of the rainbow, we decided to take a real trip over to Duppy's, the northernmost point on the coast of Barbados, a Garden of Eden with monkeys, parrots and tall tropical mountain cliffs.

There were fifteen or twenty of us, half local surfers and half American surfers, and we were all tripping our brains out. We were sitting in heaven on earth, watching twenty-five-foot mountains of water over a quarter of a mile out. It was pure beauty. We sat there for hours, watching nature's power and listening to her crashing waves, as well as the symphony of monkeys and birds chattering and singing behind us.

The party went all day and into the night. The mountains were melting and the colors brilliant. As the bonfire on the beach was blazing, many locals joined us, half of them girls. There was a little country store in the valley of Bathsheba called Rip-off's (I guess the prices were a little high on beer, eggs and live chickens) and one of the owner's many daughters was there. She eased up next to me.

"You the birthday boy?"

"All seventeen of 'em."

This introduction lasted all night and it was island style. I discovered brown sugar was just as sweet as white sugar.

That whole day and night was a birthday I'll always remember.

It was now a month since I arrived in Barbados and Christmas was not far off. Some of the Americans were talking about a great way to get halfway home, the *Federal Palm*. This ship stopped at almost every island in the West Indies, dropping relatives off and picking others up to take them a day or two home or to see other family members. It also carried mail and fruit from island to island.

For $52 I could take a fourteen-day trip to ten different islands throughout the West Indies. They sailed at night and docked at a new port almost every day, exchanging mail, goods and people. For that $52 I would sleep on deck with the locals.

I gave my surfboard to Sea Cat, one of Bathsheba's local surfers who was pleased with the gift. It was hard for them to acquire surfboards and visitors were the only chance they had to get one.

I now had a sleeping bag and backpack and a ticket ready to go.

I boarded in Bridgetown, Barbados, was going to stop at ten islands, with the last stop the most northerly one, Jamaica, where I would disembark and then fly to Miami. Boarding with me was Doc, the only other white guy on board. It turned out he knew a lot of people I knew on St. Pete Beach.

The *Federal Palm* was a great call. The stern of the ship was about half the size of a basketball court, with a little store-type kitchen in the middle with steel picnic tables and benches.

The whole stern railing was lined with a bench for passengers to sit or sleep on. About the second or third night out, we picked up a load of people and critters. Seas were about six to eight feet. The ship was a'rolling and a lot of people were a'puking, and I was finding my way to the roof of this place. And there I was, all alone under the stars, wrapped up in my sleeping bag. With the rocking and rolling of the ship I had no problem falling asleep.

Each day, a new island. I checked them all out, walking through the small port towns, experiencing that they all were different but somehow still the same. We had to be back to ship by sundown so I didn't really have long. On some of the bigger islands, I took a taxi for the day, traveling around looking at the beauty spots, which were many.

At some islands just a few people boarded. At others, the stern of the ship would be so crowded you had to sleep sitting up. There were babies crying, cats, dogs, hogs and crates of chicken making a racket like I'd never heard before. Thank God for the roof.

As the days went by I began to meet some of the crew, who were mostly West Indians. They were great people and invited me up to the forward cabins where they lived. We drank rum and I listened to their stories. I had a lot of laughs and fun with that crew of the *Federal Palm*.

About midtrip, in St. Thomas, we picked up more people, two of them white, a girl and a guy. The ship was very crowded after picking up in St. Thomas, so I spent almost every night on the roof of the stern. My new friend Doc tried once, had a hard time getting up on the roof, and once he was up there, didn't sleep well. There was no railing, and he was scared of rolling off into the sea.

While down below, mingling with the people and just taking in all the sights, I made a new friend—the white girl.

After a day or so, she became very friendly and asked me about the roof. I told her I really enjoyed it much more up there. It was quite the ride, lying up with Mother Nature under all her stars and the moon, watching the white caps peel off the swells. There were no lights, just moon and stars. I could marvel at the scenery much better than down below with all the people and lights. On the roof I felt like a free spirit flying fifty feet over the open ocean and under God's given heaven. *Bingo!* That was all she had to hear.

That night at roof time I slipped up with my sleeping bag and backpack-made pillow. I had been in my bag about five minutes when I heard, "Steve, Steve, can you give me a hand?" And up came a sleeping bag and a very pretty white girl. We spent a few nights together in pure ecstasy, drifting on the swells, fifty feet over pitch black seas and under sky-lit lights, breezy and refreshing, a harmony that's hard to explain.

I was quite the gentleman, although we did sleep in one bag using the other as a cover. Each night she became friendlier and friendlier.

I lasted as long as I could. By the third night, my male nature called. Boy, those nights were really something special.

Until Doc came to me one day when he was down below. "Steve," he said, "what the hell are you doing?"

"Whatta you mean, what am I doing? Just what any red-blooded guy would do."

"Her brother's going nuts. He's telling me his sister is going to get married in Jamaica. They're going to meet her fiancé."

"Fiancé? She's sure not acting like she's on the way to meet up with no fiancé!"

"Well, they are. He says both their families and lots of friends in Jamaica are heading to Port Antonio on the north coast for a big wedding."

"So what am I supposed to do about it?

"I dunno, but he's sitting down here with me every night and he's keeping me awake with his worrying about his sister." Doc looked me square in the face. "You got to stop what you're doing, whatever it is."

Now I felt like the cat that ate the canary. Thank God we'd be in Jamaica soon. Although I hadn't fallen in love, I was, admittedly, waist deep in lust. Just to have a good-looking woman lying next to you, cruising through the night, over the seas and under the moon and stars is quite a loving feeling.

I wonder if she ever thinks of me.

We landed in Kingston, the capital of Jamaica. When Doc and I got off the ship, we looked for a taxi to take us to the airport. The port was filled with locals running up to us to sell us all types of things. Palm hats, fruits, hammocks, parrots, wood carvings. You name it, they had it. And then some dreads (the locals with those long locks of hair worn down their backs) approached us with paper grocery bags.

"Hey, mon; mon, wha happenin'? You look here, brother. Me have something special for you."

"No, no, I'm all right."

"Come on, mon. Yum want to try the kind ganja? It's strong smoke, broda. Try the ganja. The kind ganja."

What the hell's this guy talking about?

The long-haired dread pulled out a long, fat bud from his bag. I stopped in my tracks. His hand was wrapped around a bud that completely filled his palm.

"Here, mon. You take the ganja to the States with you and smoke the kind bud."

"I can't do that. I'm on Air Jamaica to Miami and then I go straight through Customs. It's a sure bust. No thanks. But, hey, what are you selling it for, anyway?"

"Bro, give me ten dollar US. You have the bag. It's yours. Take it to the States with you, broda. Smoke the kind bud."

"Hey, hold on. You want what? Ten dollars for that whole bag?"

"Sure, bro. Yum give me ten dollar. It's yours."

Now he had my interest. "How much pot can you get?"

"All you want, mon. Yum can take it to Florida and sell it for the big money."

"Could you load a boat?"

"Yes, mon. No problem. My broda is policeman."

I asked his name and where he lived, told him I was a fisherman and would come back soon.

When I arrived home and back at our hangout on  Eighth Avenue, Pass-A-Grille Way, St. Pete Beach, I found Mike the Mullet. He was, of course, unloading two to three thousand pounds of mullet out of the little wooden kicker boat he'd built himself and from which he ran a few hundred yards of gill net on a daily basis.

Mike was a serious businessman. By now he was one of my best friends and had an unseen power about him.

He took control of conversations, and control of business transactions and just scared the hell out of most people with his Charles Bronson wolf-piercing eyes.

We loaded up his Ford pickup and headed for the fish house at Ellsworth's in St. Pete, South side.

"How'd your surfing trip go, Bo?" he asked, once we were on the road.

"Man, it was like nothing I've ever done. You should have seen the swells. Shit! You should've been there for my birthday. I had one helluva party! Everyone in the area was there."

"Your usual partying?"

"Yeah; what'd you expect? But let me tell you about the Jamaican ganja.

"I met a Rasta in Jamaica who told me he could supply me with all the reefer we wanted, that the island was overgrown with it. 'No problem, mon,' he said. I told the dread I was a commercial fisherman. He told me, 'Come down in boat.' That he has the police in pocket, that there's no problem to load a boat or refuel it and was talking eight to ten dollars a pound."

"That's it! Let's get a boat or build a boat and go down and get a load," he said.

I could see my goal in sight.

At the time, Mike was constructing and putting together a shrimp farm just northeast of the third tall bridge at Bunces Pass going out to Fort DeSoto Park. Any money he was making off mullet he was investing in a shrimp farm and a bay shrimper named the *Bait Bucket.* He wanted to raise shrimp in a natural little cut on the southeast end of Tierra Verde. He enclosed the cut with a wire mesh fencing that allowed the natural waters to run in and out with each tide. He didn't need pumps, filters or mechanical equipment that if stopped, would kill all the shrimp in the farm. Plus, they could breed, hatch and live in their real environment. The bot-

45

toms of the enclosures weren't fake or artificial. It was God's given mud and turtle grass for the little critters to thrive on.

Now he saw an opportunity to add to his ideas. Mike was on go.

He had his dreams set on a Lafitte Skiff made in Louisiana. The hull he wanted was twenty-five feet long with over a ten-foot beam, usually made for bay shrimping in the bayous.

The handful of guys Mike borrowed money from to pay for the boat and the big block gas engine it would take to put the vessel together, had no idea what he really wanted the boat for. He was a closed-mouth businessman; most of the investors who helped him out were under the impression the money was for his shrimp farm.

When the boat was finished and arrived in Pass-A-Grille, it was the ride of the beach.

We had a giant inner tube that was pulled behind the boat at 40 mph and it stripped the britches off the guys and the tops off the girls. You hung on for dear

life plus every stitch of bathing suit or cut-off blue jeans, with the banging wake jumping, flopping, aerial-snatching contact we made with the rushing water as we hit. It was great fun that summer. We dove, shark-fished and took the boat for trips offshore to catch grouper, which could not be done in the smaller kicker boats that we used for fishing on the flats.

The skiff was big and wide and ran strong with a speed that would get you to where you wanted to go.

Mike had himself a fine-built skiff and we were going to go down and get some of that ganja from Jamaica.

The problem was, with all the extra investments by all the extra guys, we were going to have to bring home a good amount of weight. The boat was only twenty-five feet long, and almost totally open, with only a very small portion of the bow enclosed. A couple of hundred pounds, at most, would fit up under the bow. And then the fuel range.

I helped Mike build a wooden fuel box at Pete Johnson's garage on 12th Avenue and Pass-A-Grille Way. This would help for the fuel range somewhat. As for electronics, Mike had a compass.

"You know Hub can shoot a sexton," Mike said. "He'd be a good navigator."

"Yeah, he'd make sure we got down there and back."

Hub, a good friend of ours, was the son of Wilson Hubbard, the owner of the Eighth Avenue Pier, Hubbard's Fishing Pier, where we all hung out in Pass-A-Grille.

Mike had all his plans made. "Let's go down sometime around the holidays," he said.

The sooner the better as far as I was concerned. I was really looking forward to this trip.

Everything seemed to be falling into place and then one morning, Mike didn't show up.

"Where you suppose Mike is?" DeeDee asked me at Morgan's Drugstore.

"I dunno. He'll show up."

But he didn't show up. Neither did Hub. Or Jimmy, my childhood neighbor who lived across the street from me. They were all missing from the beach.

"Where the hell are those guys?" Denny said. "Don't suppose they left without you, did they?"

"Hell no. Mike wouldn't do that. I'm the one who told him about the Rasta with the dreads in Jamaica. I'm the one with the contact."

But secretly I was wondering if he hadn't done exactly that: left without me. I found that hard to believe since we were such good friends, I thought. Mike wouldn't do that to me.

But he did. Mike and Hub and Jimmy did take off and go to Jamaica in that little bayou boat.

They had slipped out of town and headed south. Half the beach was talking about the trip that no one was supposed to know about.

Later Mike told me they cruised down through the Bahamas, and on their longest leg, from the Bahamas to Jamaica, he was concerned about the fuel range. But they were in luck. They got towed down behind a much larger vessel. On the way back, they ran into some bad weather and ran off course.

Straight into Cuba.

HE WAS IN luck again. They ran right into Guantanamo Bay, the U.S. naval base. Mike was so slick he could slide on barbed wire. He ran into all those problems with that twenty-five foot flat-bottomed, gas-engined, mullet boat and still came home with the load.

Mike paid for his boat, and took care of the people who had invested in it. "But I'll never do that again," he said. "This next time, we're going down with a boat that can bring back some real weight that will make some real money."

I did make some money off that trip and bought a twenty-six foot Lafitte Skiff from Rocky Rocco, a local guide and stone crabber. Rocky's slip was right next to Mike's new skiff at the High & Dry Marina in Pass-A-Grille.

Once that load hit the beach, however, we weren't the only ones talking about a bigger boat and the money that lay at the end of that rainbow.

In fact, four locals went down soon after and ran into a slight problem: two of them got busted as they waited for the boat. The other two got away.

Mike and I heard they were sentenced to hard labor, busting rock in a lime quarry in Kingston. In the meantime, though, one of them, we heard, was hospitalized.

Big Jim was at the quarry. "Let's take a boat down and do a gig," Mike suggested, "and break Big Jim out."

I was young and dumb and it was certainly something I was willing to do. We talked about it often as we planned our next trip.

In the meantime, it was nice to have some money. I didn't know how many Christmases Mom would have left, so I wanted this one to be special. I had to argue with her to take almost anything, but eventually, she gave in.

That Christmas was lovely at my mother's house. It gave me one of the best joys I've ever known to pass finances to Mom so she could get her hair done, one of the things she always loved to do, and to pay off all her household bills, afford a Christmas tree and gifts for her loved ones.

SUMMER WAS SOON in full gear. Mike and I lived next to each other in a duplex and were always doing the same things together: fishing, girls, diving, eating out at our favorite steakhouse or seafood restaurant, and of course, talking about a bigger boat with a larger load. Another trip was number one on our priorities.

We had our hearts and eyes set on a nice boat that was for sale. It was only twenty-eight feet long but had a hell of a beam. It was handmade by Mr. Paloose, the father of Greg, a friend of ours. It had a cabin, flying bridge with twin steering—one above, one below—forward sleeping berth, head, galley and table. There were also twin diesels and some of the latest electronics. To beat all, her name was the *Lucky Lady*, just what we needed. And she was docked right next to the High & Dry Marina where Mike and I docked our boats.

Our skiffs were almost identical. His was 25' long with a 10'4" beam; mine was 26' with an 11' beam. Along with the marina came a long-time buddy and one of the best mechanics around, Mannie, who was on a KOA standby around the clock. He was on go at the drop of a hat.

We had quite the set-up at the marina. Everything just kind of fell into place. The *Lucky Lady*'s slip was fifty feet behind our skiffs. We were definitely in the Luck Family.

All we had to do was walk fifty feet on the sea wall to the next dock and we could be on our mother boat, ready to fix whatever needed fixing, to load whatever needed to be loaded, and just slip out when the time was right.

While we talked about our next gig in a bigger boat, we spent all of our free time on the mile-long finger one block wide and the main street, Eighth Avenue. Eighth Avenue, also known as Eighth Street, was one of the smallest business blocks in the country. It had a post office, supermarket, restaurants, a tourist attraction, Hubbard's Fishing Pier, Laundromat, art gallery, drugstore and soda fountains, bars—plus apartments to rent—all on one small block of beach setting. On one end of the block was the beach; 200 yards to the east was Hubbard's Pier on the bay. And in between the bay and the beach there were sometimes more than a hundred kids roaming the block. Everyone called them the Beach Crew.

The Beach Crew swam the beach and pass, shot snook under Hubbard's Pier and had them cooked up at the Sea Horse Restaurant, drank ice cold beer, played foosball and pool while everyone ate fresh cooked snook, then left the air conditioning to sit on the sea wall and soak up the rays like turtles on a log.

Or we'd form a group of a dozen or two-dozen guys and blond-haired babes to stroll down the beach. If too lazy to stroll under the blazing hot sun, we could always be sure there'd be a couple of dozen kids hanging out at Jim Morgan's Soda Fountain or the parking lot alongside his store next to the post office.

I used my boat more than I did my pickup. It was faster to reach people who lived on the water. Plus it was sweet cruising with those big-breasted girls who just had to take off their tops. Pass-A-Grille was the hangout of many fine women, as well as tons of marijuana and millions of dollars. What a place to grow up.

AS MIKE AND I drove to our duplex in Gulfport, we discussed our plans for the future we had set before us.

"Mike, let's do our own trip, with our own boat. The *Lucky Lady* is a sweet vessel. We know her history, the builders and the materials she's made with. Plus, she's right in our own back yard."

Mr. Paloose wanted $14,000 for her.

"Can we keep her at your dock until we're ready to take her to her new slip this fall for charter?"

"No problem," he said. "That'll be fine, boys."

I gave Mike five thousand dollars and he put in the nine thousand remainder to seal the deal. The *Lady* was put into new ownership.

This was pure happiness. We now owned our own boat.

This sure as hell cut a hole in my pocket. I had to make some more money so I could buy my share of weed to put on the boat. Plus there were supplies to get for the trip.

Everyone was talking about a pop festival in Atlanta that was supposed to be bigger than Woodstock. Luckily the funk pot was getting ripe for reaping. Yeah. Funk pot.

A couple of locals, Big Bill and MG, told me they were interested in a funk pot trip. I told them I knew where it grew and I had a press to block it with, too. MG rented a van and we were off to Red Oak, Iowa.

I wasn't going to return to the beef master and his owner with the slow, slow tractor. I had another spot picked out close by in Red Oak. We could be up there, cut it, and dry it in the fields the same day. No motels this time. Do everything out in the fields. Load our van and be headed back to the kilo press. We would then be Atlanta bound.

It was a game plan. If I could make ten or twenty grand with a funk trip to the Atlanta festival, it would be a good start for me to have my part of financing our *Lucky Lady* trip.

Two days after leaving St. Petersburg and driving straight through, we were in Iowa. MG dropped Big Bill and me off and went back to a state park nearby to go to sleep. Late that afternoon he returned to our meeting place.

We loaded the van with garbage bags of fairly dried hemp buds. MG then drove most of the night while we slept, then changed off drivers while he slept. Five days after we'd first left, we were back home making two-pound blocks wrapped in meat wrapping paper.

We still had almost a week before the Fourth of July festival in Atlanta when I learned of another festival in Goose Lake, Michigan five weeks later. Mike Knight decided he'd make the Goose Lake festival trip with me, but not Atlanta. This would give us ample funds for our *Lucky Lady* trip in the fall.

THE ATLANTA CAMPGROUNDS were much like Woodstock, with hundreds of thousands of people stoned out of their minds, walking around butt naked, tripping, selling drugs out of vans, tents, cars, and makeshift stands looking like fruit markets. Lovemaking, too, was rampant.

It was another week of my life I was certain I'd never forget, making thousands of dollars while getting laid, stoned, and tripping out to the best music and musicians in the world. What a way to live, I thought. Often.

I came back with another jar full of every drug known to mankind and about $13,000. Mike had about five thousand dollars put away for the *Lucky Lady* trip. With my ten thousand, it was now fifteen thousand dollars we had toward the trip, but still not enough.

She could hold over a half a ton of weed and we weren't going down to bring home a pound less. Mike and I talked with Chaz, who had made the Woodstock gig with me last year. Our next trip would be Goose Lake and what Mike and I made on that, we would put toward the fifteen thousand dollars to support the *Lady*'s trip.

Sounded like a great plan, for us to have enough money to do a real load, mo' bigger, mo' better.

We didn't have a lot of time until Goose Lake, so Mike and Chaz and I brought the press and paper along with us on another trip to Iowa. Once again we arrived at the field, slipped in and cut, while Chaz waited at the state campground until late afternoon to pick us up at the meeting point.

We made another three-foot bed of funk in the van and headed right to New Hampshire where a friend of ours, Shelton, lived on a farm. We'd block it there and then head to Michigan.

If Mike and I could make ten to fifteen thousand dollars apiece, along with the fifteen thousand we already had, we'd have thirty-five to forty thousand dollars to do our Jamaican load, and the Rastas would be cutting the fall crop in another thirty to sixty days. Things were right on schedule.

MICHIGAN'S GOOSE LAKE pop festival was a long journey from Pass-A-Grille, Florida. We parked in the middle of an ocean of people ready to party and get high. Not a better place on earth to sell funk pot than here. And all parties involved in the transactions would be leaving happier than a cat in a fish house. From my past two pop festivals, I learned that with the music and partying came a multi-million dollar drug business offered to the thousands of drug-thirsty people running around with pockets full of get-high money.

Mike, Chaz and I were set up with a three-foot bed of blocks in the van, just as on our Woodstock gig. Chaz would carry the blocks under the trusty poncho while Mike and I walked in front of him making deals. By the time we made camp, the festival was already in gear. Mike and I decided to stroll through the sea of people and look the layout over before making a move, while Chaz stayed with the van and got some shut-eye. We cruised the area, taking in all the sights and sounds. Along the way Mike met a guy selling peyote buttons and chocolate mescaline.

"I'm an Indian," Mike told him, "and peyote is at the heart of my heritage." He bought a handful of buttons.

An hour later we were talking to the Great Spirit.

We sat on top of a hill above a road of moving people.

"Bo! What's that plane doing?"

"Which plane? I'm getting trails off the first one. I see about fifty of them. All different colors."

"Dumb ass. There's only one out there."

"Who's a dumb ass? I see at least fifty!"

"No, there's only one out there," he said, pointing to the sky. "Watch the gas it's letting out over the people. It's got to be the government gassing all the hippies."

I squinted until I saw just one plane. Damn if I didn't see the gas after a while. And it was definitely the United States Government at work. We were glad to be up on the hill.

By the time we figured that the government gassing the youth of America was just a part of our peyote trip, hours had passed while watching trails of colorful planes, and ribbons of people melting like ice cubes on a hot summer day.

Our peyote trip came to an abrupt end when I looked across the road and recognized Harry and Denny, beach boys and heavy in the pot game. Mike and I walked over and found that they were selling funk pot along with two or three other Pass-A-Grille groups of the Beach Crew. We had Florida friends all over Goose Lake doing the same thing we were. After talking with our friends and finding it so unbelievable to run into people from the beach, all the way up here and in this huge crowd of people, we headed back to Chaz and the van to get our business rolling.

We worked the people the same way it was done at Woodstock; Chaz with the poncho and arms of weed, while Mike and I walked in front making deals.

Blocks flew out of the van and our pockets filled with cash. On the night of the fourth day, Mike and I were advertising our deals when three black dudes approached us and asked to see a block.

They followed us back to Chaz. I retrieved a block from him and showed it to one of the men.

"This is kick-ass stoney pot. Two fifty a block."

"This is a kick-ass pistol and it'll stone you dead. Give me what you got," he demanded. "Lemme have it all, right now, all of it!."

As the other two approached Chaz and drew down on him, up came the poncho and out came an armful of blocks, thrown right at the two holding the guns on him.

We were all ass and elbows down the road, leaving them a pile of funk pot bricks to pick up and enjoy what was left of the festival.

We'd sold just about everything and had less than a dozen blocks left and our money for the *Lucky Lady* trip was in pocket. We made plans to get the hell out and head south. Before leaving, we freaked out our neighbors by giving them the remainder of the blocks we had. They kept thanking us as we eased out of the campground and headed south.

Now back in the burg with the money to furnish a trip, Mike and I started making plans for the biggest load ever brought into St. Petersburg Beach. The summer was ending and the fall right at our doorsteps. The fall cut in Jamaica was at hand, a perfect time of the year to get the best product and buy a good load.

We rigged the *Lady* with necessary additives, charts, and extra fuel capacity. We checked all the electronics. She had a refrigerator, built-in live bait well, two diesel engines and all the comforts of home. We even went to Sears and bought a garbage compactor for compacting our load, along with fifteen hundred packing bags. This should be a pleasure trip and one hell of an adventure.

After buying more supplies, a blow-up Zodiac raft for loading, food for weeks, plenty of dive gear, fishing gear, oilers, jackets, blankets, pillows and all the homey things one misses when offshore, our boat and supplies were ready.

As Mike and I went over our plans and course of travel, we decided to make it a four-man crew this trip. The two additional crew members turned out to be Carlos Gerdes and Harry Hoffman.

Carlos was born in Venezuela and lived in St. Petersburg most of his life. He was a great sailor, in the Navy, a close friend, and had money to buy his share of the load. Carlos was mellow, a Latin-lover type, dark tan with straight jet-black hair. He was the oldest of us four. (I was the youngest.)

Harry was from Michigan, and had moved down to the beach to join up with his life-long friend, Denny Caughey, also from Michigan but who had lived in St. Petersburg most of his life. Harry lived on a houseboat at Blind Pass Bridge. The Michigan boys were the northern market. They could move all the weed that came in.

In fact, Harry had the load sold before we even received it. He had money men on standby, so it was wise to have him along. He was also a one-in-a-million guy.

Harry was a bouncer, bodyguard and professional arm wrestler when in Michigan. He weighed about 375 pounds, had a baby face and actually a round body shape like a fat little newborn baby. But the stealth, raw power that lay hidden within him was breathtaking. He was one of the strongest men I've ever set eyes on.

Harry's personality was just the opposite; he was kind and gentle. And by no means a seaman. He couldn't even swim.

Well, we had a hell of a crew: a Latin lover, a snowbird that couldn't swim, and two salty mullet fishermen, who all grew together on the little Florida island, getting ready to smuggle three-quarters of a ton of marijuana into Florida. The profit would be better than a quarter million dollars. This reefer business was stepping up.

It was now fall and a lot of the finance money had been spent on families, and supplies. And just plain *spent.* So we set up a payment plan.

Each crewmember got a certain amount of weight he could buy with his own money and that share of weight would be his payment.

We also had three guns on board with boxes of ammo. This had nothing to do with our business—we didn't feel the need to carry guns in the reefer business, where everything was trust, handshakes and smiles (except maybe sometimes selling it, like at Goose Lake). However, it's expected that all oceangoing cruises have firepower aboard. Mine was a nine millimeter, given to me by Albert and Ronnie, long-time partners and my secret investors in this gig.

We also figured we could use the guns to cut the boredom, shooting at coconuts and flying fish. We hid them under a drawer on the bottom floor that had a perfect space for the guns and bullets.

Our plan was to take the *Lucky Lady* down the west coast of Florida to the Okeechobee Waterway, then east to Stuart, then head on to Freeport in the Bahamas, and island hop our way to Jamaica. The return would be the same, but with fewer stops; we'd be too anxious to get back and peddle our goods.

The four of us gathered at the marina late one night. With everything in order we were finally getting ready to be on our way. We slipped out in the early a.m.

It was a clear, starlit night with clouds off to the east that turned into a God-sent sunrise with orange, reds, pinks, and a greenish background and that turned into a light blue sky. As the bright light of the sun began to rise, we were headed south past Venice. The water was crystal clear with miles of white bait. The dolphin tore the sardines up from the bottom as the birds bombarded from above. It was a cool, crisp morning filled with adventure and excitement. I rode on the bow with my eyes missing nothing. I was filled with a spirit of life and wondered what Columbus must have felt like.

The *Lady* was a slow boat, but had many comforts I've already mentioned. We could all sit comfortably in the well-built galley out of the wind and ocean spray. With the advanced electronics we'd invested in, it was reassuring to know where we were going, and that we would stay on course with the automatic pilot.

We passed the beautiful white sands of Captiva Island running along Sanibel's awesome view of Florida at its best. Then headed to the Caloosahatchee River where we began a breathtaking trip through the hipbone of Florida, waterfront property with horses, cattle, gators, hogs, turtles, snakes, armadillos, eagles, ospreys, buzzards, cranes, egrets—just to name a few. Natural beauty that most people will never see in Florida.

It took all day passing the locks of the Barge Canal. I could have taken years crossing it. Many parts we passed seemed to me as if I was the first person to set eyes upon the area. It was unchanged Florida as it has been for hundreds of years. And the waterfront houses and cattle ranches with mega yachts tied up to joint docks were captivating.

We hit Stuart just after dark, docked at a hotel on the water and checked in. We all got a good night's sleep.

Early the next morning we filled up with fuel and bought any last minute needs and headed South-Southeast to Freeport. We were deep into the Gulf Stream an hour after daybreak.

It was a cold, windless morning, a mirror slick ocean surface with bus-sized ground swells rolling in from the north. I was lost in amazement at the size of the swells.

My ride was in the flying bridge, surfing the *Lady* deep into the troughs of the waves, then climbing to the tops of some of the set waves that put me ten to twelve feet above the trough, only to surf back down into the valley of these deep, glassy ocean mounds where I sat high in the flying bridge, looking at the tops of the giants at an eye-equal distance. It was a roller coaster ride, smooth but scary, without a drop of water entering the boat. The swells were transparent, crystal clear. Schools of fish surfed through the dark, deep blue liquid that rolled south to unknown beaches that only Mother Nature knew.

We spotted land in the late afternoon and pulled into the east end of Freeport and a Bahamian officer boarded the *Lady* and looked carefully around. He entered the main compartment and stopped.

"What the hell!" he exclaimed when he spied the Sears compactor and the fifteen hundred bags.

"Oh, that?" Mike said. "We're bringing it for a Bahamian friend who lobster fishes. He needs to compact his bait."

"Oh, yes mon," the official said, smiling and nodding. "Very nice."

All was cool, once he heard we brought gifts for a Bahamian.

We docked in a yacht basin and slept on board.

Freeport was full of excitement—women, parties, fine seafood and beautiful boats.

Partying on the boat with the women friends we met in Freeport was like musical chairs. We met girls day and night. The problem was trying to get them alone on the boat without the other three guys coming aboard while alone with a nice tanned body in the forward berth. We were like dogs in heat. If one of us had a woman on board, it was like a magnetic pull for the other three to have a need for something on board.

We finally showed respect and worked out a system with leaving a towel off the flying bridge, meaning on-board sex; sex in motion.

We were all in love (except for Harry, who had Linda on his mind). We thought we'd died and gone to Heaven. But after three days of sex, partying and spending money, which we didn't need to spend, it was time to leave.

It was time to press on to Jamaica, the land that would make us millions.

We headed due south to Staniard Creek, Andros Island, about a hundred miles away, give or take a rock's throw, and steered clear of the temptations in Nassau. Freeport was almost enough to bankrupt us; we certainly didn't need to get into more trouble in Nassau with addional partying.

On the way down, the wind picked up out of the Southeast. At this time of year it meant only one thing— in a day or two the wind would switch to the North and we'd be enduring a cold front.

The wind did switch. The barrier reef around Andros was a solid wall of water and the *Lucky Lady* was on hook in the little bay; how long depended solely on the weather.

"DAMN, IT'S BEEN two days, Steve," Mike complained. "Harry and me are thinking about flying back to the burg and—"

"You're what?"

"Thinking about flying back and picking up some more charts. Might as well use this time for something. We're sure not going anywhere. This wind won't lay down for at least a few more days."

I looked at Carlos; we both knew. "Yeah. Right. Get some more charts. Like we don't have enough? You mean get some pussy, don't you? And leave Carlos and me here alone to watch the boat."

"Well, if you want to look at it that way. Someone has to watch the boat."

We pulled anchor and eased over to a small dock and seawall on the south side of the bay. They left. Carlos and I returned to the middle of the little bay and anchored the *Lady* once again. We settled down on this twenty-eight foot wooden box to wait it out.

TALK ABOUT BORING. Carlos and I were going nuts, trying to cut the boredom by fishing water that was full of sharks and barracuda driven up into the little bay by the storm, and large waves on the outside reef.

It didn't help much.

When I couldn't think of anything else to relieve the boredom, I pulled out my pistol, cleared the clip and started cleaning it.

I pulled the trigger and when a bullet flew between Carlos' legs, barely missing his hand, blew through a cabinet, passed through three shelves, the floor and finally into the hull, I realized the gun wasn't empty.

"What the fuck?" Carlos yelled. "What you trying to do, man?"

"Damn it, I cleared the clip. I didn't know there'd be any bullets in there. Jeez, I'm sorry. I didn't realize. Damn, I'm sorry."

Suddenly I thought about the shot.

"That bullet! *SHIT!* What if this hole goes all the way through the hull?"

"Fuck! You think there's a chance it did?"

"Don't know, but I'm going down there and check it out."

I put on my mask and fins, dropped into the milky colored bay and was immediately surrounded by thousands of 'cuda, some of them six feet long. This was as bad as the gun going off.

The mask to teeth confrontation took out any air I had in my lungs, and expelled it to the surface with the rest of my body following right behind. The bay was full of the swarming fish, pillaging in the shallow water for weak prey. I'd just be another meal. But if the *Lady* took on water . . . Carlos and I'd both end up victims to the 'cuda. I had no choice but to go back in.

On my second dive, I confirmed that the bullet hole went all the way through the hull. Thank God though, the wood had swollen and the hole closed up. There was no leak.

But the hole in the galley sure didn't close up. I knew I'd never hear the end of this one.

I had to get off the boat. The more I looked at that hole, the more I worried about what Mike was going to say. Carlos and I decided to brave the cloudy water, and swim the short distance to shore. With each stroke came the thought of all the schools of shark and barracuda that were just below me. Once ashore, we walked to a little shack a half-mile down the road. Old Bahamian men played dominoes while we had a few hot beers. It was nice being on dry land for a while, talking to someone else instead of just each other, but we were ready to get on with our mission. The swim back was much easier with all the beer in us and I never once thought of sharks and 'cuda. The next day Mike and Harry finally returned, and we picked them up, moving the boat for the first time in almost a week.

I was nervous as a whore in church.

Once Mike was on board, the issue was not the bullet hole.

"Lamb, how many people you tell about this trip?"

"What do you mean?"

"Shit, as soon as I got back on the beach, Albert and Fox were asking where you were and if we'd already done the trip and got the load back. What the fuck's that all about?"

Shit! I was screwed. "I was a little short and didn't have enough for my full part of the load. So I made a deal with them and borrowed a few grand."

"They're back in the burg, Steve, waiting on their pot and we haven't even gotten loaded yet! Who else knows?" His stare made the 'cudas look like goldfish.

"Mike, I didn't tell anyone else. They're my partners and good friends. I just wanted to be able to buy my share of the load. If anyone else knows, it didn't come from me."

I looked at the others and no one met my stare. After getting my ass chewed out by Mike, the truth was revealed. Everyone on board had silent investors back home. So much for our "secret trip." We were the talk of the town. In fact, half of the beach was waiting on us, like Santa Claus at Christmas time.

FOUR

ONCE THE TRUTH came out and all the bitching was done, it was back to plotting a course and setting a time frame.

The next day the weather cleared but not the milky water and the big swell on the outside of the reef. We decided to stay in the little bay for just one more day and let the water clear. We'd be on our way the next morning.

We planned on heading to Great Exuma, to Georgetown. A little less than a hundred and fifty miles south/southeast, we should hit it before dark. We'd top off with fuel there and spend the night on what would be our last island stop in the Bahamas before we were on our way to Jamaica.

The next morning it was still a mess on the outside, so we had to run inside of the reef, which was very dangerous and slow going because of the shallow coral heads just below the surface. The *Lady* drew three and a half to four feet and there were spots of coral not shown on the chart all along our way. We could sink in a heartbeat. So we ran the boat from the flying bridge and with someone standing lookout on the bow.

Our estimated cruising time was more than doubled. We'd be lucky to make even South Andros by night.

We eased along all day just over idle speed, backing down many times just short of dry coral beds. We crept into the night with Mike operating and Carlos swinging a spotlight from the bridge. Harry and I were lookouts on the bow. Suddenly I saw a boil of water just yards in front of us.

"Mike! Back her down! Back her down! There's dry reef right in front of us. We're gonna hit it. Back it down! Carlos! Hit the light!"

Once the water was lit, all I saw was a thin cut of boiling water rushing through a bone-dry coral bed. The cut was less than five yards across. We were caught in a funnel of water being sucked through the reef.

Harry fell to his knees holding onto the bow rail. "Hold on. We're gonna hit the reef!" he shouted.

I was right next to him, hanging on for my life. I didn't know whether to shit, shave, or wind my watch. "We're gonna run aground!" I yelled. "Hold on, hold on you guys."

Mike had the diesels singing a frightening song as he backed the *Lady* down. The light that Carlos had been holding was now rolling around the flying bridge, like a searchlight after war planes. As the *Lady* shook and shivered, we somehow slipped through the ribbon of water that split the giant bed of coral heads. The more Mike backed down, the faster we went forward. We didn't have a foot on either side of us as we shot out the other side of the reef. Neptune treated the *Lady* as if he'd squeezed a wet watermelon seed between his trigger finger and his thumb. You could have skied behind our boat. Who managed that?

It should have been the end of the trip. And the end of us.

But it wasn't.

We made only forty miles that day, finally docking that night up a little creek at an abandoned dock and hotel on South Andros. We now had about a 110-mile run to Georgetown (with God willing) in all deep protected water. Our estimated time of arrival should be just after midday. We'd leave at the first of light.

The trip from South Andros to Georgetown was a pleasure, in clear blue and turquoise water filled with flying fish sailing off our bow and porpoise surfing our wake. We entered the Exumas right on schedule and picked up a hundred gallons of fuel—all we were allowed because the fuel ship was late and fuel was short. We'd have plenty for the run to Great Inagua tomorrow.

Our problem was we were short on food, but since we had tanks, spear guns, rods and reels, heavy poles for bottom fishing, and light gear for surface jigging, we fished and dove that afternoon. The *Lady* had a built-in live bait well in the stern as big as a bathtub.

We'd found a nice protected little spot just off Williamstown, the southernmost end of the main island in the Exumas. There was a large shot of coral named Hog Cay just south of us. We explored that area with the bottom machine, passing a break of bottom that started at 40 feet and had ledges that fell to 100, 110 feet deep. The walls were stacked with fish.

Carlos, Mike and I strapped on our tanks, grabbed our guns, and fell overboard. Harry swam like a rock, so he stayed on board.

The visibility was top to bottom. If there was a heaven on earth, we were swimming right through the middle of it. The walls of coral had colors unknown to life above the surface of the earth's ocean. As I dropped along the painted walls of beauty, I passed through schools of fish that swished and turned and weaved and swam between each other, showing off their God-given hypnotic beauty of colors and swimming grace. There were fish of all sizes—tropical fish, snappers of many varieties, grouper of every kind, and sharks passing with curiosity about the bubble-breathing creatures they had probably never seen before.

My taste buds went straight to the walls of lobster. I was under ledges ringing tails of lobster, putting them into my dive bag. I had a giant loggerhead turtle eating out of my hand. The grouper, snapper and sharks that were attracted by the lobsters' cries were a show in itself. It was like feeding bread to seagulls on the beach. Each time I threw a lobster head into the current of the crystal clear water, it was a football game of turtles, eels, grouper, snapper, and a lone shark to see who would receive the pass as I released it into the playing field. I rang a dozen and a half nice tails and then teased a twenty-pound black grouper into thinking he was going to get dinner when the truth of the game was, he became dinner. I nailed him with a kill shot right in the spine behind the head. There was underwater life like I'd never seen. I looked over at Mike stringing up a huge carbo. While surfacing with him and a cloud of scaly friends, I watched Carlos close behind a big mangrove snapper as he made the kill shot for dinner. It was a dive of a lifetime.

We had a seafood dinner at its best, pulling out our trusty lava barbecue. We loaded it with split lobster tails, then fillets of black grouper. After the grouper, it was stuffed snapper with roe, lobster and green peas, wash-

ing the feast down with Bahamian beer and watching the sky mix up colors with clouds as another day set into the ocean. The sunset was as colorful as they get. It was definitely special, like the good Lord was producing a day just for us to enjoy. And I did.

We finished our meal, dumped the ashes and coals to our lava barbecue pot overboard, cleaned up and watched the darkness of night squeeze out the last light and colors of the day's existence. It was a nice cool, brisk night. After checking the anchor, we were all out like lights.

I dreamed that night in color.

I was up just before daybreak, had a big pot of coffee started and ready to start the day off. We were short on fresh water so it was a one-gallon wash-up shower and tooth-brushing deal. It was grouper and oranges for breakfast. We pulled anchor with the crack of day and were southbound, running on the west side of Long Island for a good part of the morning. Once passing Dead Man's Cay, the westernmost part of Long Island, it was a straight shot to Great Inagua Island. Free with deep water, we passed Salina Point, the southwestern-most part of Crooked Island, about one o'clock in the afternoon. That was our halfway point to Great Inagua. We hoped to arrive in Matthewstown for sunset.

The trip was beautiful. We had dolphins playing off the bow and riding the wake of our boat most all day. We also spotted whales on three different occasions, pods of pilot whales and two spottings of much larger animals, twice the size of our boat.

Our jump was a little over 200 miles and took us fourteen hours. We saw the light of Great Inagua not long after another gorgeous sunset. The fuel dock was shut down after dark. We also needed to buy some food and fill the fresh water tank. We anchored next to a handful of sailboats and other yachts that were moored just off the island.

The next morning we were up and I was putting fire to the coffee. It would be the last of our seafood but it would be a grand finale. I had four lobster tails and a grouper fillet left. I cut the rib cage out of the fillet and put it on our six-aught. I dropped it overboard while I was fixing breakfast. Right in the middle of our seafood breakfast the drag on the six-aught sang and the pole doubled over. With breakfast on the grill I called for Harry or someone to watch the food. I jumped to the stern, grabbed my pole and began an early morning fifteen-round bout with my opponent. I had the fish coming up, then he went down and I came up. I went down and he came up. It was a battle like I played on the teeter-totter in elementary school. I was hoisting him with all I had. I was scared of breaking him off. I at least wanted to see what I had on the end of my line. It felt like a giant stingray.

He was just sticking to the bottom and coming up and going back down. The whole cove was awake and cheering me on. The decks of the boats were full of people drinking their coffee. When I finally got the best of him and he came toward the top of the water, it looked as if I had a diver on the end of my line. As the huge grouper rolled over at the surface, Mike put the gaff to him.

We towed him over to the coral wall that was the fuel dock and the dock man and his group of children, about a dozen, helped me weigh the fish. It was a 113-pound Warsaw grouper, a beast.

We topped the boat off with fuel and filled the fresh water tanks. But the water was not the best drinking water in the world. There were no jugs of drinking water for sale and the food was short in the market. We bought a case of cereal, the last three cartons of powdered milk and piles of canned food, while the children looked longingly at the fish. The fuel man said the freight ship was almost two weeks late.

I traded my fish for ten drinking jugs of water.

I really didn't want to clean the big brute anyway. It would be like butchering a hog. I knew we could catch something a bit tastier on the way to Jamaica and we wanted to get on our way.

The father and his kids jumped up and down and thanked us for their giant fish. Everyone was happy.

It was still before noon and time to head for Jamaica.

We had to hit the windows between cold fronts. The north coast was about 250 miles of open ocean, with the point of Cuba about fifty miles south. In four hours we'd be in the windward passage and rounding Cuba. By midnight we'd be half the way between Cuba and Jamaica. Our plans were to be off the Jamaican coast by early morning.

We were all electrified with the thought and excitement now that there was no turning back.

FIVE

WE'D EACH TAKE two-hour shifts to operate and run the boat. In the flying bridge that beautiful day, I was surfing the *Lucky Lady* in three to four foot swells with a following sea. I was supposed to be holding a course on the compass that would run us almost eight miles off the east point of Cuba. However, I had an urge to run west of that.

"Run the number I gave you!" Mike yelled up to me. Not just once or twice, but numerous times. It was so hard not to move in for a closer look.

"Damn it, Steve. Keep on course. You're heading too close to Cuba. I don't want to go through that ordeal again. Keep your eyes on the compass, damn it."

Not long after, we spotted buoys, Bahamian or Cuban lobster traps. It didn't matter which; we had no meat at all. Powdered milk, cereal and canned beans needed something to go with them. And that live bait well in the stern was just waiting to be filled.

There was a ledge coming off the deep ocean blue to twenty fathoms, strung with lobster pots and not a boat in sight. As we pulled the traps full of tasty lobsters, we filled our live well. Nothing like fresh lobster for the trip from the ocean's own supermarket.

But these were some poor fishermen's livelihood.

We didn't want bad karma, so we stuffed the bait cups with hundred dollar bills, U.S. money, three times what they'd collect taking the lobster to their home port. We prayed the karma would do us right, and wondered what those fishermen would think.

After my watch I pulled a half dozen of the fat lobsters out of the live well, split them and put them on our trusty lava barbecue and we all indulged in a delicious lobster dinner.

We ran throughout the night and into most of the morning when we spotted birds overhead and coconuts floating in the water. And now there were more weed lines; land was not far off. By midday the horizon was dotted with dark green mountains, whose peaks were lost in the clouds that surrounded them.

As we got closer, it was a landscape made for a *King Kong* movie, wild, plush and mountainous.

But now that we were here in Jamaica, we realized that foolishly, we had no game plan. Mike, the ingenious and fearless thinker that he was, quickly devised one.

"Me and Harry—we'll fill the army bag with clothes and cash. My magnum, too. You can drop us off."

"Yeah, that sounds smart," I said, "ever hear of Jamaica's Gun Court? You get life for possessing a single bullet! And while you're at it, just where you intending to go? Who you going to see? You got any idea? What about my guy in Kingston?"

"There are way too many people there," Mike said.

"This is the country. This is where they grow it,"

"You know anyone over here?"

He nodded. "I know a cab driver in Ocho Rios."

"Okay. Make sure you find some fuel, too." *Dumb ass* quickly entered my mind. We were definitely a boat-load. Here we were, all the way down to Jamaica, float-ing around on a little boat with not enough fuel and in a hurry with no one to meet. "Where you want to be dropped off?"

"Dunno, but we'll find a place."

The only thing we all knew was that whatever we were going to do, we had to do it quick. We had to make a decision and run with it.

We decided our drop off point would be on the North coast, the isolated side of the island. Mike and Harry would go ashore, make a connection and buy the herb. Carlos and I would go around the east side of the island and head south, where we would top off with fuel in Kingston. The following day, we would come back, pick them up, and head back to the good ole U.S. of A.

We entered a small lagoon and pulled up to a make-shift shack at the end of a rickety pier. I halfway expect-ed Tarzan to walk out on that old wooden dock. Though he didn't appear, a few of his native friends checked us out from the thick overgrowth and through the coconut trees growing along the beach. Mike and Harry, with the overstuffed army bag, jumped off the boat and onto the dock as if they owned the land.

Leaving Mike and Hoffman to go and do their thing, Carlos and I eased out of the bay, and took a Loran reading of our location so we'd have no problem return-ing. It was early afternoon. It would be well after dark when we entered Kingston.

The seas were good-sized but we made good time. However, once turning the point and on the south coast, everything changed. The hills and mountains of Jamaica were full of shops, buildings, airports, and life. I guessed that's why no one was on the other side of the island. Everyone lived here. Although it was now night, the mountainside was full of lights from the houses there.

We pulled into Kingston Bay, a giant bay, and had no idea where we were going. Our Jamaican chart showed a yacht club on the east side of the bay, so we headed in that direction. It was very dark and the shipping channel was not well marked. We figured out where the club should be and headed that way, then came to an abrupt stop, with our engines screaming. We backed off all power. *What the hell is going on?*

"Hey, mon, wha' happen?" An old man in a dugout canoe, with a wax candle on the bow for light, came paddling over in the pitch black darkness. He had to be 110 years old and he lit into us like a swarm of killer bees. "Me net! Me net!"

After mellowing him out by giving him some hot beers, I put on my mask and fins and was overboard. By the time I had all the net released from our props, the little old man had enough of our beer in him and he was now our best friend in the world. He pointed the direction of the yacht club. "Don't go straight, mon. You'll run aground; go 'round the point."

We thanked him for the information and were on our way.

We pulled into the so-called yacht club and found it closed for the night. The place was dead. So we tied up and we waited for the morning. Once again, it was going to be Carlos and me, waiting on Mike and Harry.

Carlos pointed out the phone on the outside wall of the clubhouse.

"We could call a cab, get a little reefer, eat a nice dinner," he said. "Maybe even get laid."

"Fuckin'A, now you're talking. Sounds good to me. We'll be back by morning and ready to head out."

When the cabbie arrived, we asked for his help.

"No problem, mon. My brother has the best ganja on the island and plenty fine good Jamaican food and a lot of womon, broda. Womons, womons, womons."

We jumped in the car and sped off down the dirt highway on our way to the capital of Jamaica.

He took us to a bouncing part of town. "Go with my brother. He'll take care of you," he said and winked.

We went to places I never knew existed. He drove through the poorest parts of the city, definitely the asshole of the world. And then he turned on to a four-lane highway lined with fine clubs and restaurants.

It had changed one block to the next, like night and day. We ended up at a club in a fair to partly cloudy spot of town, the only white guys in the place. The cab driver brought his brother over to meet us.

"Go with him," our driver said. "He'll take care of you."

That we'd left the boat suddenly washed over me as a big mistake. What if we're robbed? Killed? High-jacked? Damn! But we had no time to change our minds.

The brother was driving a sweet, brand new Jeep, one like you'd find back home. I figured then he must be all right, driving this nice vehicle.

"What's on your mind?" he asked.

"We want some smoke," Carlos said. "Get something good to eat and a few ladies."

"You'uns come with me. I'll show me white brothers the Jamaican style. Come on."

We got in the Jeep and he pulled out a bread bag full of buds that had to be a pound.

"Give me fifty dollar for the weed, brothers, and I'll be your driver all night and take you to your boat when you want. You'uns pay me what you think is fair."

"Shit, Carlos, what the hell we gonna do with all that weed? Mike will know we left the boat."

"It's a long ride back to Mike and Harry. We'll roll a bunch of spliffs and throw the rest overboard."

But they don't have rolling papers in Jamaica. Everything's rolled out of paper bags.

We rolled a big fat spliff, and were stoned right nice. Cruising around in that open Jeep, I felt like the president. And very white.

People were everywhere and our driver explained that many of them were without homes. Kids and women, and along with them, cats, dogs and hogs, roamed the streets. My mind changed about wanting a woman.

We turned onto a main street and continued cruising along.

"The Police!" the driver yelled. "Hold on."

We hauled ass through streets and alleys, just missing people, pigs, donkeys and dogs.

What the hell's going on?

Here we are, a pound of pot, pockets full of money, and no papers of entry. Damn!

The driver definitely knew his way around. He turned off the highway and cut across a swampy field. With the police now out of sight, we flew into a box type garage and pulled down a plywood door.

"This is my woodworking shop," the driver explained. "You can stay here for the night."

"No," I insisted, "we have to get back to our boat."

"Not safe," he said. "The police see two white boys, and they will shake you down for money, drugs. Maybe worse.

"You sleep here in my shop. I have some couches. You want to carry back smoke? I have good cover. I can fill these footrests full of ganja and put herb in wood carvings, and you can take them to the United States. Customs will not know."

"No, thanks, pal. We're just fishermen and we need to get back to our boat."

"Mon, tonight is not safe."

So Carlos and I spent the night in a makeshift wood-carving studio, a garage-type house made of plywood and cardboard. It was a long day and very good ganja. We fell fast asleep.

SIX

WE AWOKE THE next morning to the scratching, low rumbling sound of voices and laughter. I opened my eyes and saw the three surrounding walls of patched plywood, cardboard, and gaping holes. Through the holes, I could see a dozen or more little black faces watching us.

Carlos and I started to stand and half of them ran away in laughter and screams.

It was then that our driver entered. "You ready?"

"Sure are," I said.

"Good. Many people know the white men are here. It is time to go, mon."

I agreed a hundred percent. We loaded up in the Jeep.

As we drove back to the dock, I was praying we'd have no more encounters like the one last night, seeing we had no papers or stamps on our passports, plus the bread bag of weed on the floorboard between my feet.

We arrived back at the yacht club about ten o'clock. It was a different scene from the deserted docks of last night. We went to the boat and stashed the herb under the drawers in the galley.

The dock master approached when he saw us.

"This your boat?"

"Yeah. You got any fuel available?"

"Sure, mon, if you have your immigration papers. May I see your papers, please?"

"C'mon, can't you let us have some without having to show you papers? We'll pay good money."

"Strict rules. You can go across the bay to the Immigration Office in the industrial port and get your papers," he said with finality. "You clear there, you can have all the fuel you need."

Time for another plan. We decided to go on ahead to the industrial port where the cargo freighters dock, but without a visit to the Immigration Office. We *were* going to buy fuel.

We pulled the *Lucky Lady* alongside a cargo freighter, but when passing it, we forgot to lower our two antennas along the flying bridge. *SNAP!* They caught the bow line that tied the ship to the dock.

"Oh, shit! There go our electronics."

Carlos immediately checked; none of the electronics worked. Suddenly, I felt like I'd been kicked in the gut. I could already imagine the anger in Mike's eyes.

But despite this damaging problem, the deckhands at the port had no problem selling us the 300 gallons of fuel we needed. And didn't even ask if we had immigration papers.

We left the fuel dock and headed across the bay, back to the open water for the long ride to the drop off pier. It seemed like the perfect time to smoke a joint.

I sat down at the galley dining table and was rolling us a couple when I noticed a fast approaching white boat heading straight toward us. I grabbed the binoculars.

"POLICE!" I yelled.

"Fuck!" Carlos exploded. "They're too close to dump it overboard! Dump it in the head!"

While the *Lady* was slowing down to an idle, I looked through the porthole in the small bathroom as the police boat tied up to our starboard side. I stuffed the weed down the toilet, pushing it repeatedly, but the whole pound kept coming back up.

What the fuck could I do? I pulled the whole roll of toilet paper off the wall and wiped the wet, dirty bathroom floor with the clean, white paper, making it look as shitty as possible, then stuffed the dirty paper down the toilet so it covered the weed. I dropped my pants and squatted just as the door flew open. I was cross-eyed and straining, grunting music as the officers barged in on my bare ass. They caught me and nature in the middle of a date.

I jumped up, grunting, with a toilet full of nasty, dirty paper behind me, and two Jamaican police officers directly in front of me.

They'd seen enough. "Finish your business, and get up on deck," one demanded. I exited the head a short time later, and one of the officers immediately entered behind me. There was only the shitter to check, and my black brother didn't want to play in there.

Once on deck, they held us at the stern of the boat as they searched the *Lady*. They opened all the drawers of the galley cabinets, but never pulled out the bottom one where the guns and ammo were hidden. Another blessing from the Good Lord. But they did find the Sears garbage compactor and fifteen hundred bags. This raised an eyebrow and was reason enough for the authorities to take us in.

Once inside the bay, we entered a marked canal and pulled up to a dock with four slips at the harbor station where Carlos and I were taken. Although we were separated, we were taken into two different, but side-by-side, rooms. Luckily the construction was so shoddy I could hear everything Carlos was asked. And his answers.

It was very late in the afternoon and getting dark outside. They checked the boat's papers and called the States for information.

"Who is the owner of the boat, this Michael Knight?" one officer asked.

"A longtime friend," I answered. "We rented the boat from him. For a month long vacation in the islands." *The same answer Carlos had given.*

None of the officers wanted to take the time to drive us down to Central, fill out the paperwork, and check the papers on the boat again. The lead investigator asking the questions received a call from home and was obviously eager to get out of the station. "They have a tank full of lobster and plenty of room on board. I'm not getting them dinners and a bed. They can cook their own food and sleep on board."

My heart jumped for joy.

We were marched back to the *Lucky Lady*.

"Stay on board until morning," an officer ordered. "We will deal with you then."

As the evening lingered on we could see and hear officers leaving the building. It seemed as each hour passed another light went off and every now and then, a boat would pass behind the station, but aside from that, it was pretty dead.

"You know, Carlos, to be on the safe side I'm dropping these," I said as I dropped the pistols and ammo overboard. "I ought to clear the toilet too, but there's no way to clean it up."

Carlos nodded in agreement. "Yeah, and you know, this is our chance to get the hell out of here."

This time I nodded in agreement.

We quickly untied the lines and pushed off the last piling with all of our strength. The boat quietly drifted as if on tiptoes. Then it stopped.

"Crank the engines, Carlos," I whispered. The engines came alive and the *Lady* eased her way out the canal and toward the shipping channel.

The boat came to an abrupt stop, as if she had stubbed her toe. *Shit!* Here we were, escaping from the harbor patrol and run dead aground. Right behind their building! I jumped over and pushed her free. Praise God!

Cautiously we ran with all of our lights off into the dark, unfamiliar territory. It was just before midnight when we reached open ocean. We pushed the throttles up to running speed.

"It'll take all night and into the morning," Carlos said, "before we can get to Mike and Harry at the pier."

"Yeah. We've got no time to waste."

"But what about the harbor patrol when they find us gone? They're gonna shit."

"Damn, Carlos. You know they're gonna have the word out all over the island."

"And they've got Mike's name."

"His name? What about our names? They've got the whole nine yards. They've got our names, the name of the boat. They called the States to find out all that information when they were interrogating us." The more I thought, the sicker I got.

Carlos felt as sick as I did. "What if they're loaded? They'll be waiting for us in the States. Let's go back empty."

"Empty? We've gone this far, Carlos. We've gotta come home with a load. Shit! I owe people back there. We all owe somebody somethin' for this gig."

"To hell with the money, Lamb. I don't want to end up in a Jamaican jail. They'll be looking for us all over this island."

Carlos kept stomping his foot, a move he only made when things weren't right.

We ran west into the darkness throughout the night until the sun began to throw rays of light on the horizon behind us. As a new day crept up, we were now on

85

the north coast. All we could see were bays and cliffs repeated up and down the island.

"Carlos, the coast all looks the same. How we gonna find 'em with no electronics. Can you get anything at all on that Loran?"

"Not much. We lost almost everything when we snapped our antennas. All I've got is the number where we dropped 'em off. The signal's not good and everything looks the same."

I wracked my brain trying to think of a landmark. "I remember passing Dunns River Falls when we were headed to Kingston to refuel. I saw it on the chart and it was about two hours from where we dropped Mike and Harry off. Let's head west until we see the river and then figure about two hours after."

Two hours after passing the river we had no luck in finding the bay. We ran back and forth, up and down the coast just wasting fuel we didn't have to waste. Fuel was now becoming a problem on our minds.

"We can't keep running like this," I said. The swell was large so we stayed a good ways offshore. It was going to be hard to spot that little wooden dock. "Damn, I can't believe we don't have the Loran. I didn't take any land bearings at all. What do you want to do, Carlos?"

We turned the engines off to save fuel. We needed to come up with a game plan, which was a hard thing to do with no sleep since yesterday and the constant thought that the police could have their eyes on us at this moment.

"Let's ease a little further out," Carlos suggested, "then turn the engines off and try to get some sleep."

We tried that, but the pounding swells and the ever-present fearful thoughts refused to let this happen.

We were once again just off the coast in search of the little wooden dock in the little lost bay.

About midday, we were so close to the coast our boat surfed the backwash off the cliffs and reefs.

"Hey, Lamb! There's the little dock. Shit! This is the bay right here."

"It damn sure is!"

We entered into the bay and cruised toward the dock where Mike and Harry were supposed to be waiting for us.

They weren't.

We idled in the bay and waited, and waited. And waited. Finally we turned off the engines and dropped anchor in the middle of the bay, not wanting to ever lose this spot again. Now, in addition to the thoughts of what would happen to us if the Jamaican police caught us sitting here, I started thinking what might have happened to Mike and Harry. *Did they get busted on shore with the money? How will we ever know? And Mike had his .44 Magnum with him. Shit, if they found that he'll never see day light.*

That afternoon a small plane dropped in the bay just twenty or thirty feet off the water and flew right over our roof. *It has to be the feds.* It kept dive-bombing us, checking us, all afternoon. Carlos and I had nothing but questions: *did the pot get busted along with Mike and Harry? . . . are they on our ass and sending a Jamaican boat for us? . . . shit, should we leave while we're still free and haul ass to the U.S? . . . but we can't! . . . we can't leave Mike and Harry; they're still on the island . . . what if they got busted here waiting for us and this plane is radioing in on us? . . . SHIT! . . . we're stuck; we have to wait for them . . . Mike'll leave word if something's happened, won't he? . . . but what if all of Jamaica's after us.* And on and on it went.

We stayed in the bay. Had to. We had no fuel to waste and couldn't leave our friends.

"We'll stay right here 'til they return or we hear news of what's happened," Carlos declared. "Or worse yet," he continued, "until the Jamaicans drag us off in cuffs."

I was praying for the first part; that Mike and Harry would show up.

We spent the night in the bay, sleeping off and on, just waiting for a Jamaican gunboat to pull alongside. Dawn broke. It was a new day. And we were still alive and free. But still no Mike or Harry.

"Carlos, what are we gonna do?"

"We're staying!"

At eight o'clock the frigging plane started again.

"This has to be surveillance, Carlos, keeping an eye on us until they can get a gunboat here. They've got our ass."

"We have to find out something before we're leaving. If they've got Mike and Harry then we're just sitting here until they come get us."

"Yeah, it's not like they don't know this boat and who we are. Nothin' we can do but wait."

SEVEN

JUST ABOUT MIDDAY, a local in a canoe paddled out into the bay toward us. We didn't know what to think. As the canoe came closer, a little Jamaican dude yelled out to us.

"Lam, Lam, is there a Lam on board?"

Shit, he's calling me.

"Lam, I bring news from Mike and Harry."

We hung off the side of the boat to help the man onboard. "Where are Mike and Harry?"

"Your friends could not make it yesterday. They have not found the mon. They will be here this afternoon and they want Lam to come ashore and find the mon with the ganja."

The law's looking for us and we're in serious trouble and now I'm supposed to go ashore and look for ganja? Fuck!

"We can't stay here, man. This plane's been flying over us constantly for two days now. It's the police. They know this boat and they know us."

The man grinned broadly. "No mon! Not police. This be crop duster. You think police?" He laughed. "He spray for da bugs on the banana trees. Many banana trees on the cliffs. This dock belongs to the St. Ann's

Parish Police," the man said. "It's all right for you to tie up here."

Tie our boat up at a police station? Load our marijuana at a police station? "Nope. Don't want to do that," I said.

"No, dem closed. They only open every couple days. You will be okay here."

"I'm not buying any of it," Carlos said. "They haven't found a connection yet? They haven't been back here yet? We're loading up at a police station? No way that's happening. Plus I'll be damned if I'm staying on this boat again by myself."

"Carlos, I promise. I'll go into the hills. I'll find an herb connection myself and be back as soon as possible. We're a lot nervouser than we should be. Thinking a crop duster's the feds! Hell, they probably don't even have word over here about us leaving Kingston."

"How can you be so sure?"

"How'd they know where we're at? Hell, we spent the night in the bay. This is our second day here. If they knew we were here, we'd a'known about it. A crop duster! A fuckin' crop duster!" I laughed. "Let's get 'er loaded and get outta here. Just wait one more day. Hang in there."

"How the hell do I get stuck on this boat every time?"

"Carlos, you are a captain and you were in the Navy. You're the finest Venezuelan I know."

"Cut the shit, Lamb. I'm the only Venezuelan you know! Go back with them, but you better be back tomorrow."

IN THE LATE afternoon, Mike and Harry showed up on shore in a car. I jumped in and we took off to a nice hotel on the ocean where they'd been spending all their time.

Harry was pissed. "Mike's been cruising around in the car," he said, "but he won't stop and talk to anyone. He's paranoid as hell."

"We've got to find the right person," Mike said. "We're talking about a lot of weight and a lot of money. And I'm not fucking paranoid. I just don't want to spend the rest of my life in Jamaica."

"We couldn't figure out what happened when we reached the pier and you weren't there. Let's head for the mountains to make a contact," I suggested. "Let's get this deal going."

As we drove up into the clouds, Mike passed by several Rastas without stopping.

"Stop, Mike. You know he smokes herb and knows where to get some."

But Mike drove on, passing all of them, continuing further and further up the little, narrow, winding mountain road.

Finally a big Jamaican with dreads stood by the side of the road. "Stop the car!" I yelled, "He's who we need to talk to. Stop, damn it, stop!"

Mike finally pulled over twenty yards past the man. I jumped out and ran back. "Hey, brother. We're looking for some reefer, ganja," I said to the dread.

"No problem, mon!"

We both got into the back seat. As soon as the doors were shut, Mike turned to the Rasta. "Take me to your boss. We want to buy some serious weight and we will take care of you for setting it up, but we want to talk to the man you work for."

"Yes, mon. Straight on, straight on."

He directed us a good ways up the mountains until we came to Murray Mountain where his employer lived. He told us to stop and park the car in front of a building and follow him in.

The dread was a soldier and worker for the owner of the mountain dwelling, the "King Daddy" of the herb business. We all entered, and a young black bro brought us three Red Stripe beers and told us to sit down and make ourselves comfortable. About twenty minutes later, an older, well-dressed man with a New York detective-type hat strolled in from the back.

"Boobs Campbell," he said, extending his hand. "And just who are you guys?"

"Mike, Steve and Harry," Mike said.

"Are you hungry?"

"Always," I replied.

"Come, we will talk over meal."

We followed Boobs through a doorway to the back of the building where we all sat. And then a pleasant, nice lady that Boobs introduced as his wife, 'Miss Dolly,' asked, "Would you boys enjoy some souse?"

"What's *souse?*" I asked.

"A Jamaican soup made from pig's knuckles," Boobs explained. "It will make you strong and healthy."

"NOW WHAT'S ON your minds?" he asked, as we finished the pig knuckle soup.

"We're looking to buy fifteen hundred pounds of marijuana," Mike said. "We have a boat down on the coast. We need it loaded so we can take it back to the States."

Boobs smiled broadly, his face shining with happiness. "I have been waiting for you many years," he exclaimed.

"I prayed that one day the white man with a boat would show up. You three answered those prayers. How do you want the herb?"

"All buds," I said.

"No, mon. I mean, you want to buy it or do I front it to you?"

"What's the difference?"

"You pay cash, it's ten dollars U.S. a pound. Truck delivery you pay five dollars a pound more. I front it to you, it will cost you twenty a pound plus five dollars a pound to truck it to the coast."

"We'll buy it. Here's fifteen thousand." Mike pulled out a bag wrapped in tape and handed it to Boobs. In trust.

He put the bag by his side uncounted, in trust.

I then told him we had a compactor with fifteen hundred plastic-lined paper bags so we could pack much more ganja on board. "But we've got to get it off the boat. You can keep the machine, Boobs. It's for you for further trips—we intend to come back."

That piano keyboard of a mouth glistened at us, all white on black.

"No problem. I send Yulsie with his truck. He will follow you."

"But how will we get the bags and compactor off?"

"The police. They will take it off for you. No problem. Cyrus, my good friend and partner, he is chief of St. Ann's Police. But I will need another three thousand to pay for the police services and protection."

He was passed another stack of bills to cover it all.

We discussed, over the rest of Miss Dolly's savory homemade Jamaican meal, the details of how we wanted the herb. We agreed that Boobs would compact it into twenty-five-pound blocks and we'd take delivery the following day.

Yulsie followed us out of the mountains, down through Alexandria and through Brownstown, all the way to the coast at St. Ann's. We showed him where our boat was anchored.

"Okay," he said. "Now you follow me."

We followed Yulsie about seven or eight miles down the coast to a dockside restaurant and bar. It was now dark. He told us to bring the boat to the dock at the restaurant. He would wait.

I got the little guy in the canoe to take me out to the boat. I was on my way with Carlos to the restaurant in yet another bay seven miles to the west where we tied up alongside a waterfront restaurant and dock. We unloaded the compactor and bags with plenty of help.

Including Cyrus, the chief of police! My thoughts finally turned positive when I saw that without a doubt, Boobs had the police on the payroll.

"Now you pull up at the end of the dock," Yulsie said. "No problem with the boat there, mon. What's your hotel and room number?"

Mike told him.

"Go to your hotel and me soon come. Then we'll go

to Salem Beach and I will show you where I will load you tomorrow night."

It wasn't long before Yulsie showed up at the hotel. We followed him to a large sugar cane field at Salem Beach where there was a deep drop-off coming right up to a natural coral ledge where we could pull our boat within a few yards of the wall. It was a well-protected spot and seemed like a fine place to load.

We told him we would be anchored right off there tomorrow night and be waiting to see him with the herb. He told us he would have a small, wooden canoe to shuttle all the blocks to us. This trip was finally coming together. Or at least, I prayed it was.

"God, I'm glad to finally be off that boat and on solid land," Carlos said on our way back to the hotel. By the time we arrived it was almost nine o'clock and the tiki bar on the beach was blasting reggae music. What else could we do but stop?

"Let's get something to eat," Harry said.

That sounded good to me. "Hell, while we're at it, why don't we have a have a drink or two to celebrate?"

Wouldn't you know: two pretty Jamaican ladies swayed over to us at the bar and asked if we would like any ganja or sexual pleasures. Well, hell, yeah. We decided we could use a little of both and headed for our room. Things were turning for the good.

A couple of hours after the girls left, Harry was pacing the floor.

"Hoffman, what's wrong?"

"I need to get out of here. I'm catching a flight tonight. Or the first one in the morning. Back to St. Pete."

"You nuts, or something? What you talking about?"

"I'm married, Steve."

"Yeah. What else is new?"

"No, damn it! I mean, I'm *married.* I've got a wife! What am I doing this shit for? I did Linda wrong." He buried his face in his hands and I could barely hear him.

"I had sex with another woman." He looked up at me. "Don't you understand? I can't do this to her. I gotta get home!"

"Harry, take it easy. First of all, you got no entry into this country."

"Don't care. I gotta get home to Linda."

"Well, how's Linda gonna like it when you end up in a Jamaican jail? Huh? Whatta you think is gonna happen as soon as you try to buy a ticket?"

"I got to try it. I've got to get home! Don't you understand?"

"Sure, I do," I told him, though I didn't, but we talked and talked and finally he chilled down.

We came *this close* to fucking up the best deal we ever had.

The next morning we had a nice big tropical breakfast in a lush jungle setting full of long-tailed Jamaican hummingbirds and songbirds.

This was the big day. God willing, we'd leave tonight and be headed for the United States. Harry was still wanting to leave, to fly home and talk to Linda about his 'affair' and we wanted to keep him occupied until we got him back on the boat.

We hung out at the hotel until late afternoon, then turned in the rental car and took a taxi to the waterfront restaurant where the boat was tied. With the sky sharing its prettiest colors for a beautiful sunset, we had good feelings about this at last. The sky was mostly red— 'red sky at night, sailors' delight.' We climbed aboard and started the boat. A little after dark we anchored off the spot at Salem Beach and eased the stern of the *Lady* within yards of the rock ledge and settled down to wait. And wait. And wait, some more.

I couldn't control my thoughts. Did we get ripped off? Did Boobs get busted? Are we going to get busted? As midnight came and passed, we once again began to wonder what was going on.

"Hope we don't get a repeat of Kingston."

"You think the Jamaicans called the States?"

"Think they're gonna be on the lookout for us?"

We finally fell asleep. I awoke about three o'clock. Carlos was up. "They haven't showed," he said.

"Damn! Shit! Think Boobs is going to rip us off?"

"Looks that way," Carlos said. "Sure fuckin' looks that way."

"Damn! It's going to be daybreak in a few hours. He'd better show."

In spite of our worries, exhaustion took over and we must have fallen asleep again. Just before daybreak, I heard a voice.

"Mon! Mon! Hey, mon!"

We jumped up like jacks-in-a-box at that Jamaican accent and looked out from the stern. Yulsie was in a small wooden canoe. He handed us a rope attached to one end of the canoe. The rope on the other end was held by a Jamaican on shore, standing next to a truck.

Cyrus the police chief came along, too. Yeah, baby: the police loading our boat. I liked that thought.

They loaded the canoe with 250 to 300 pounds of nicely wrapped blocks of ganja and then we pulled the canoe to our stern and unloaded it. Then Yulsie and his men pulled it back and loaded it again. Back and forth the canoe went.

We stuffed the *Lucky Lady* full of blocks. The Sears 25-pounders took over the entire forward berth, the head, and the galley. Except for a small hole for the lower steering console, the entire cabin was crammed with weed. We had this twenty-eight-foot cabin cruiser stuffed. We'd have to sleep on these heavenly beds of herb and then crawl to that steering hole when it was our watch. It was nuts. We were packed on a boat of marijuana like sardines in a can.

We yelled thanks, and promised to return, then headed off the north coast of Jamaica.

We could see the mountains of Jamaica until mid-morning, but by afternoon it was all deep blue ocean without a thing in sight.

Our thoughts turned into words.

"What are we gonna do with this load? We can't come in the States like this. You know the Jamaicans have called the authorities."

"We're not coming in loaded," Mike said. "We're going to unload in the Bahamas somewhere and come in with a clean boat, just to see what happens. We'll cruise right up the coast to Stuart and if there's any heat on us, we'll definitely find out. Better clean than with a load."

We slowed our running time down to hit Great Inagua the next night, where we had to visit our little buddy with all the kids, our fuel connection.

With the *Lady* full of blocks, we'd have to slip in after dark and pay him a little extra to go down to the fuel dock and top us off at that hour. Since the fuel fill was on the stern, we'd drape a tarp off the flying bridge to hide the herb somewhat.

The following night we eased in, woke our buddy up, stuck a few Franklins in his hand and told him we needed fuel at the fuel dock immediately.

"No problem, mon."

WE HEADED NORTH/NORTHWEST out of Inagua, wanting to stay to the west side of the Bahamas as much as possible. The weather was beautiful. Passing South Andros, we headed for the east side of the Florida Straits. Thank God we had an ocean current on our stern since we were running short of fuel.

Once again our figuring was off: There was no way we could make Florida without fueling up again. But how could we stop with all the pot on board?

Southeast of Andros we began seeing small rock islands. We spotted one with an old abandoned radar shack built up on poles. Mike wanted to stash all the pot on a rock out in the middle of the ocean in this little wooden shack with no roof on it.

"We'll go back into Andros and top off with fuel," he said. "Then run into Islamorada clean. It's just over a hundred miles west of where the radar shack and our pot is hidden. If there's any word out on us from Jamaica, we'll not be carrying any contraband. We'd come in with a clean boat. What could be easier?"

We topped off at Fresh Creek on Andros with a clean boat and headed back toward our little island, passing it and heading onto the west to the Islamorada bridge. We rented a slip at the marina just inside the bridge, across from the Holiday Inn motel. We rented two rooms there, took a real shower, and all of us were in dreamland.

All of us but Harry.

That big baby-faced bull was ready to hitchhike, walk, take a plane, taxi; it didn't matter. He was going to St. Pete to ask for forgiveness from Linda for the whoopee he had down in Jamaica with a call girl. Now, what the hell's on his mind? What's wrong with this Yankee?

Harry was making such a ruckus about getting to St. Pete we were all up. There would be no dreamland today.

We were on the phone immediately. Mike called a few of the silent investors and he also called Denny, Harry's partner. Denny talked with Harry and mellowed him out somewhat.

We decided to unload right here in Islamorada's pass. Just on the other side of the marina, they were starting a housing development, and the mangroves and marshes were all cleared back and graded with dirt roads coming straight to the inlet. And after dark, there was no one around—a perfect place to unload.

We called Denny again and my friends, Charlie the Tuna, the owner of the pool hall, my boss at one time. (Oh, how things change.) And Albert, my long-time friend and silent partner who gave me extra cash for the trip. They would come down with their drivers. We would unload into their vans, big trunk Lincolns and Caddies right next door. All contacts would be made at the Holiday Inn and we'd move from there right after dark.

By the second day, everyone was in place. Half the beach boys from St. Pete Beach were in the Keys somewhere close to the Holiday Inn. Mike and I met with our people and they had their drivers in place. Denny had a driver take Harry back to his wife where he could go to confession. Carlos stayed and was going to organize the drivers for when we returned with the load the following night. The radio channel was set up with Carlos to check at the top and bottom of the hour, starting with the first hour of dark. We also had a backup channel to switch to if needed. Our plan was to stay in radio contact with him, but only when we were nearby, because due to our broken antenna poles, we had only a ten- or twelve-mile range.

Just before daybreak, though still dark, Mike and I headed out the Islamorada pass with our two new crew members, Charlie the Tuna, and Albert, and began our 200-mile round trip. We planned to be back just after dark.

The *Lucky Lady* was under the bridge and eastbound in the dark of a very early morning. The *Lady* was cruising on God's own liquid mirror—the surface of Mother Nature's ocean was breathless, without a breeze. It was as if we were skating on ice.

A few hours after light the water turned from a deep dark blue to a light turquoise color. Not long after that, I spotted dark shades of color beneath the surface—coral reefs in the shallow water. Small rock islands began to appear. We passed on and saw an island that showed on the chart to be one of a chain. A little further down the rock chain, we ran into another one. When we reached the third one, and it wasn't ours, we really missed the Loran. We spent a few extra hours looking for our wooden shack on a rock in the middle of the ocean. And then finally, we spotted that shack standing high on four wooden legs, the shack filled with our precious product that would make us all much richer young men.

By now it was midday. We tied up ten feet off the island where there was plenty of water surrounding the little rock, with an anchor off the bow and the stern tied to the nearest leg of the shack. Mike climbed into the shack and passed me down a block at a time. I passed it to Albert and he'd relay it down to Charlie on the boat who would pack the blocks. We had a great little rhythm going until Albert took a second too long to get his block to Charlie. I looked up and caught the next package of reefer square in the face from about ten to twelve feet over my head. The next thing I knew I was flat on my back looking up at Mike and Albert. Contact with the Sears block of marijuana knocked me out for the ten count.

I've heard of knockout weed before, and now I've experienced it.

After getting my senses together and the last block crammed into place, it was off to Islamorada, the last stretch of our trip.

Because we had a hard time finding the island with the shack and our stash, it was late afternoon and the sun seemed to be going down faster than normal. It would be well after dark when we entered the inlet. We had a little over two hours before hitting the Keys.

The night was black; no moon or stars at all. We had all our running lights off. We laid up high in the cabin on the blocks of ganja in a dream state of mind, drifting in and out of thoughts with the sound of the diesels humming along. Tuna and I noticed a port and starboard light far off in the horizon. "Hey, Mike. Check the lights on the horizon," I said.

Mike, at the wheel, looked out. "It's just a ship heading south. We're crossing a main shipping channel."

We fell back into a mellow state, Tuna and I sitting on blocks across from each other. We were mumbling about something when I saw a green and red light so close to the window I had to snatch my head at a 45-degree angle just to see it.

"Mike!" Tuna yelled.

By the time Mike focused out the window it was all steel bow with a wall of white water. The ship was so close the running lights were out of sight. They were over us!

A blinding light turned on searching for our boat. Mike hit the throttle, ran in front of the ship and then made 180-degree horseshoe turn and cut back right in front of a six-foot wall of whitewater and the steel bow once again.

The light followed across the ship's bow, looking for us. We slid back, missing the bow by feet. It almost flipped our boat when the bow wave smashed into us. The ship slid by so close I could touch it. God definitely had His hand in on that move.

As the ship passed, the searchlight swung back and forth looking for the debris the captain must have thought they spit out the prop wash.

"Mike, what the hell were you doing cutting back in front of that ship? We just shot from the jaws of death."

"If I didn't cut back in front of the ship, they would have lit us up like daylight. Seeing the reefer, the name of the boat, your ragged ass head of hair, they would've radioed on ahead. But they never saw us. They probably think they ran right over us."

We ran for another hour, hour and a half and finally saw the lights of Hwy. A1A. We lined up with the lights of the Holiday Inn. Then, after almost 1,800 miles of cruising, the port engine started missing, choking for fuel and then just shut down.

Great. All this way and then right at home plate, fucking engine problems. We were less than half a mile off the bridge and then the starboard engine started the same gasping sound.

We were dead in the water. The tide was rushing in. We had shallow water all around us. We started moving blocks off the engine box to make room to get at the engine. We had to hit our spotlight looking for our problem. Mike was in the bilge and our light jumped around following his every move. The diesels were starving for fuel. The problem was in the fuel line. And with all the reefer on board, we had a limited area in the engine space to work.

It was a nightmare. There was no room anywhere on board, we had little hallways through, over and around walls of marijuana. I wormed my way to the throttle as Mike investigated the fuel problems. We finally got one engine running and then the other. The boat was just about to run aground on a sandbar when we pulled back and eased off under power.

Now, just east of the Islamorada bridge, the engines started choking for fuel again. One engine died and we were left at fifty yards outside the pass in the middle of the channel when the other engine shut down. *Damn it to hell!*

The tide was boiling in. We were drifting straight for the bridge. Suddenly a bright light traveled across the boat.

"You've got to be shittin' me! Mike, it's a cop!" A highway trooper was sitting on the top of the bridge, and had swung his spotlight out across our boat. He left immediately and sped quickly over the bridge. "They've got to be on to us."

"What the fuck's going on," shouted Mike. "The engines are dead and now we've got cops waiting for us to come in?"

I turned on the running lights.

"Tuna! Take over at the controls!"

I crawled out to the stern and went to the bow. We had no power and were floating toward the bridge at a strong two to three knots.

"Steve! Hang on," shouted Albert. "I'm coming up to give you a hand."

"Shit! We're gonna' hit the friggin' bridge. Mike, can't you get an engine started? Tuna, try and crank an engine and back this thing down."

"This is my first time at the wheel. How do you start this thing?"

"Fuck, Tuna. You're as worthless as tits on a turkey. Mike, get these engines started or we're gonna' smash into this bridge."

"Steve. Get on this side of the bow with me. If we hit it's gonna' be on this side."

"Damn, Albert, it's not the pilings we have to worry about; we're gonna' hit the main span of the fuckin' bridge. Or get stuck under it—with over half a ton of pot on board this is cute . . . *cute* . . . Damn it, Mike, get an engine started—we've got to back this boat down— we're coming up on the bridge fast. Albert, get ready and try to hold the boat . . . *Not from the flying bridge! GET DOWNYOUCRAZYSONOFABITCH! You'll be crushed!*"

We were instantly blanketed by concrete but the *Lady* miraculously squeezed within an inch or two from the bridge that was the highway above us.

Praise God! A few more minutes and we would have been stuck in the Islamorada Bridge with over a half a ton of marijuana. Nice headlines.

Once we were through and on the other side, there was the trooper, sitting on the water's edge. He hit us with his bright lights and then did a 180-degree turn and raced out of the marina again. *What in the hell was that all about?*

"Mike, shit! We haven't even made contact with Carlos or anybody onshore."

"I've been in the bilge the whole time. Tuna, you've got the radio. Turn the fuckin' thing on."

"What the hell's going on with you guys?" Carlos shouted. "How come you haven't had the radio turned on?"

"Damn engines went out," Tuna answered. "We were working on 'em."

"Tuna, ask him what the hell's going on with that trooper on the bridge."

Tuna relayed the message.

"When you had your light on out at the shallows, it looked like a boat in trouble. When you entered the pass, the trooper came flying down to the marina to check you guys out. Shit, he almost ran me down. I was standing right here on the wall waiting to make contact with you. Have you guys forgot that's my job?

"After the cop hit you with his bright lights, I guess he figured everything was okay and he shot out heading south. I had Ronnie follow him a few miles. He was Key West bound," Carlos said. "We've been flipping out. Let's get these vehicles loaded and get outta here."

I grabbed the radio from Tuna. "Carlos, start sending the cars one at a time to the second point. We have to unload these fish and get them on ice as soon as possible."

"Yeah, I know. I'm watching you guys drift by me right now."

"Hey, drive over to the second finger and help us get this boat ashore."

I dove off the bow with the anchor rope and swam toward shore. Albert swam with the stern line. The tide was ripping and it was a battle pulling the *Lady* to the edge of the canal until Carlos and a few of the drivers jumped down on the sandy shore and gave us a hand.

Once we had the *Lady* tied up, the drivers that were already there started loading their cars. Carlos jumped into his truck to return to the Holiday Inn to send the other drivers to where I was at the entrance road at the second finger. I had a radio to let the guys on the boat know when I was sending down vehicles. I was watching, too, for the trooper. He still had us worried.

As each car or truck came to the entrance of the road I told the driver to turn off his lights and head down to the water's edge. A big Lincoln pulled up, and as I stuck my face close to the driver's window to give directions, my heart fell out my ass and I ran for the mangroves.

"Steve, I'm driving for Fox," Rick O'Connell, my baseball coach, and St. Petersburg Beach police officer, yelled to me. "He told me he was working with you and Al."

I slipped out of the swamp and returned to the car. "Coach, what's up? You're a cop by day and a reefer dealer by night?"

"Who better to drive a load of pot than a police officer?"

"I can't argue with you there," I said, shaking my head. "Just drive down to the water, with your lights off."

After the last vehicle loaded and was gone, headed to St. Petersburg behind at least a half a dozen others, we could relax somewhat but still had to get the boat back to the marina. Finally the port engine sipped a swig of her much-needed fuel and came to life just long enough to get us a few hundred yards back to the marina, where we still had our slip.

We tied the boat up next to the hose on the outside dock, and began washing her down. It was quiet and no one was to be seen. While cleaning the forward berth, I opened the bathroom door and, damn, if there wasn't a 25-pound Sears compact garbage bag of weed sitting right on the floor in front of me, God and the whole world.

"How the hell did you guys miss *this* one?"

I stashed it in the bushes at the housing development, went back and cleaned out the toilet that had not been

106

used since our boarding in Kingston. It still had the wet, messy pound of weed that Carlos and I had bought and almost ended up in prison because of.

The *Lucky Lady* was home in the U.S. of A., clean, unloaded and tied off securely in a nice slip in the Keys. As for me, I was laid up across the street at the Holiday Inn with the rest of my buddies. I could now finally relax. All of us were tired but too happy and too hyper to sleep.

Stealing lobsters, leaving hundred-dollar bills to have good karma, damn! and it worked, Carlos and I aren't in prison in Jamaica, chased by the police in Kingston, that Jeep, jumping curbs, crossing fields, sleeping in the wood carving shack, waking up to the giggles and all the little black faces and big white smiles, sitting on the toilet with a pound of pot below my ass talking to the Harbor Patrol, eating souse with Boobs, the main man of Jamaica, loading in a sugar cane field, whores at the tiki bar, broken antennas from our refueling illegally in Kingston, the plane buzzing our boat for two days and it was a crop duster, refueling with a boatload of marijuana aboard, playing chicken with that ship . . . *and Rick O'Connell!* Thought after thought eased across my mind until a deep, dark sleep finally took over.

The next day we checked out of the motel. Charlie Tuna rented a van. We went over to the boat and unloaded dive tanks, diving gear and odds and ends. We also picked up the almost forgotten bathroom block of reefer. Tuna headed northbound to the burg.

Finally we had the hardest part of the trip behind us. It should be downhill from here. With the load off the boat and a load off our minds, we headed back toward Pass-A-Grille, all smiles. Northbound along Florida Bay, we stopped at Flamingo Key for lunch and to do some fishing. We caught snook and redfish, then headed up the west coast of Florida. We stopped at almost every main town and port for a drink and a visit, making a one-day trip a three-day-er. Marco Island, Naples, Port Charlotte Bay where we killed the snook and red fish once again. Spending a night at Venice, fishing, fucking and having the time of our lives. Life was great. Tomorrow I'd be in Pass-A-Grille with a lifetime of memories I'd never forget. Oh, plus I'd be thirty-five thousand dollars richer when I stepped off the prettiest lady I'd ever met.

HOME SWEET HOME once again. We had made it, thanks to God, no doubt. There was more excitement in my past year than all the Sean Connery movies put together and I was paid for it. I had more cash than I had ever had in my life. James Bond and his top secret vehicles had nothing on the *Lady* and the excitement and adventure she had taken me through. Not bad for just turning eighteen.

EIGHT

ONCE THE *LUCKY LADY* was back and the money rolled in, the seed to international marijuana smuggling was planted. We had brought home sixteen hundred pounds of marijuana, more weight than we thought we had. With the trip came the stories we told our close friends—who, how and where we did it. Loose lips sink ships, but as big as our egos were, we couldn't keep quiet. And there was all that money. Over a quarter million. Everyone on the beach now wanted a taste of that honey.

But our biggest mistake was telling our friends of our connection, Boobs, the man who prayed to Jah, his higher power, for the white man and his boat to come to him. He was the money maker.

As soon as we ran our mouths about Boobs and where he could be found, a few of our friends went to him, saying they wanted to buy all his weed and they would control all the boat trips coming to Jamaica.

But Boobs was good people. "Mike, Steve and Harry paved the road for you to get loaded with me," he told them. "And now you want to cut them out? No, mon. If you want herb, you go through them, mon."

This put us in the game as the quarterback. If you want to receive, we have to pass.

I saw capabilities of making enough money to set my family and myself up for the rest of our lives. It was beyond the wildest dreams of most people.

Everyone has a dream: school, college, studying a third or a quarter of your life just to get a good job. Then working until you're old and gray and the youth and best part of life has passed. Nope. I didn't see it that way.

My heart was set on helping myself and others—some of the poorest people of Jamaica—and making them richer than they had ever dreamed.

MIKE AND I ate out almost every night at our number one steakhouse on 34th Street or at our number one seafood restaurant, Gene's Lobster House, on Madeira Beach in front of the Madeira Beach Seafood House, right next to the Stuart Causeway. We were always discussing our opportunities and talking about a bigger boat and doing a bigger load.

But a real boat costs real money and a big load costs big money. And then there were the trucks, drivers, farms, stash houses. It would take a chunk of money to do a load the size we were talking about. We were friends and partners but we started brokering loads for friends with boats and crews. Sometimes we did our own trips but still helped each other out if needed. There were many groups of people organizing different trips, but everyone still worked as a big family, one hand washed the other.

Smuggling was no longer a dream. It could be done. It was done. The herb business flowered and flourished. Hundreds of tons of marijuana and millions and millions of dollars were first put together as trips of adventure to third-world countries to import the joyous and much-wanted marijuana.

Many people knew of the product and the money being made. But the secrets of the trade were still held within a tight group of lifelong friends, mostly beach people, who went to school, rock concerts and partied together, played baseball and football on the same fields, surfed, fished, fought and fucked as friends growing up. That lifelong friendship brought trust and knowledge of each other. It was a brotherhood.

We arranged a gig on a sixty-foot snapper boat, the *Queen Angel,* a Cyrus hull, stern cabin and all ice storage from the cabin to the bow. She was just what Boobs Campbell had prayed for. Her holding box was as big as my living room. We were going to fill her belly with ten thousand pounds of salad. We'd be leaving out of Fort Myers and returning to our neck of the woods, the waters we had fished all our lives.

We gave the owner—he was also the captain who would be running the boat with us—money to get supplies he needed for his boat. We gave our fourth crew member, Mammal, a list of supplies to round up and order. Mike and I then flew to Montego Bay, Jamaica, rented a car and checked into the Playboy Club, Ocho Rios. First things first.

We left our baggage in the hotel, and carrying the money we'd brought down, were off to Boobs' house in Alexandria.

We had to wait most of the day with Miss Dolly at their home until some of his people ran him down. Later we found out that he was in the bush, buying herb. He bought a good percentage of all the ganja crop in the country and all the farmers in the region planted and farmed for him.

Plus he had his own mountain range on which he grew ganja.

We were definitely working with the main man.

We sat with Boobs at his dining room table going over our next load while Miss Dolly, her daughter and a few elderly women served us dinner along with the specialty, *chicharon.* A whole bull's head burnt crisp to the eye sockets and all the skin fried to a golden brown was brought in on a wooden slab. It's like beef jerky, pork rind, but soft and greasy. After you eat through the skin and the meat of the cheeks and head, you get to the so-called good part, the brains. A little of the cheeks was all right, but I wasn't much for the brains.

The soup, however, was great. After that, we were served herb rum, a bottle of over-proof rum stuffed with fresh-cut green ganja buds and then buried in the red clay they had high in the mountains for two months, and then dug up. The clear rum had turned to a dark green and, a little capful of that would put something on you Ajax couldn't take off.

We went over all our arrangements. B. Campbell was getting serious. He had bought a three-bedroom house with a small pool right on the ocean just west of St. Ann's shipping channel. Kaiser's bauxite plant was just inside the most inner part of the bay where big cargo freighters docked to take on the aluminum ore. It was a perfect spot to meet our boats from the States at a big buoy outside the bay. The bay and its shipping channel were easily found on any chart of Jamaica, including our buoy. It would be an international meeting spot for the future.

Our spot was a bell buoy that rang with the swell of the ocean, so loud a blind man could find it. She was a half a mile northeast of the back yard of our stash house. Boobs had two canoes that held about twenty-five hundred pounds a load.

The water was fif-
teen to twenty feet deep
straight down at a rock
coral wall where his
yard met the ocean. The
rock wall was about fif-
teen feet high and had
natural steps that were

actually ledges to get to the water. It was the tits that
fed the baby's mouth for unloading big loads to hungry
boats.

As we arranged price and weight, Boobs told us there
would be no problem with the weight. The price was now
twenty dollars a pound, more than we paid last time.

That price included sugar cane trucks to deliver to
the stash house where the load could be kept until the
boat showed up. Plus Boobs had a team and a half of
some of the biggest, strongest Jamaicans on the island,
who would unload the trucks and load the canoes for
us. Trucks, stash house, manpower, and I mean manpower, plus loading boats. Boobs took care of everything
for that twenty dollars. It was quite a deal. Oh, yes. Plus
police protection for the herb as it came out of the hills,
through Alexandria and Brownstown, and through the
sugar cane fields to the shoreline. It was a sweet, sweet
slice of pie Boobs offered us. For ten thousand pounds,
we needed two hundred thousand dollars.

"Boobs, we need half the load fronted."

"No problem, mon," he replied. "I will front all you need,
but I will get thirty-five dollars a pound on the front."

The deal was on. Nothing owed if the load got busted.
But if the load made it, we owed another $175,000 for
the front of five thousand pounds.

Now that everything was set, Mike and I returned to
St. Pete and went to a mangrove island we knew well,
a place west of Tierra Verde and just southeast of Shell

Island. We cleared a spot there for the unload. Then it was back to Jamaica with Boob's fifty thousand dollars. We'd bring another fifty thousand on the boat when we came down to get loaded. When we sold the pot, a few of us would fly down and bring the additional $175,000 to him.

"Or you can put it on the next boat," Boobs said, his smile ear to ear. "You are coming back, aren't you, mon?"

"Boobs, we'll bring you the first hundred and seventy-five thousand we collect," I said. "I don't want you waiting on another boat, but one will soon come."

We sat down and drank some rum. "Oh," I told him, "Boobs, I'd also like to order two cases of that herb rum."

Boobs smiled. "No problem, Steve. It is on the house, mon, for you to enjoy."

We set up dates and times and our buoy marker in the shipping channel for our rendezvous. If we had a problem and weren't there the first night, they should return the next night at the same time. This gave us a leeway if we were a day or two late.

We returned to the hotel. That night at the Playboy Club, Mike and I ate at the restaurant, and were served by beautiful Playboy bunnies. Later we hooked up with a few of the beauties and partied in sparkling, crystal clear Caribbean waters and under tropical palms on sugar white sand beaches. It was women and a night to remember. That night just put icing on the fact that 10,000 pounds would cost us $275,000 to buy and half of that was fronted. Our sales price at $200 a pound times 10,000 pounds would net a healthy two million dollars, with us clearing $1,725,000. Not bad for a few weeks' adventure.

We flew home the next day passing over Cuba and across the Florida Keys. The flight was breathtaking. Nature's beauty had much to offer.

We were home for two days and hooked up with Mammal, and the Captain, loaded supplies and were headed south in the Gulf through the Yucatan, past Grand Cayman Islands and straight to our buoy meeting marker in St. Ann's Bay. The meeting date was on time.

We had $50,000 on board, the remainder of the $100,000 we owed him. We had over $5,000 in gifts: shoes, Levi's, hats and shirts, and shovels, rakes and hoes for farming and planting. We had flashlights, too, things that would be of much help to the poor people of the bush. We arrived two hours after dark and there was no need for a radio. Yulsie was in a boat tied up to the bell buoy, waiting for us.

We followed him in to just a hundred feet off the natural coral wall where another canoe and a group of big, strapping Jamaicans waited. We filled the canoes up with our gifts from the States. Mike and I went ashore and met with Boobs, gave him the other fifty thousand. He handed me two cases of herb rum. I talked with him. We laughed, hugged, shook hands. It was all smiles, and I was off in the next canoe with a boatload of marijuana headed for our boat.

We had the *Queen Angel* loaded in four hours. Her belly was full but our cabin and sleeping quarters were free of any pot, unlike the last trip on the *Lucky Lady* where we were sleeping on blocks of herb. This load was all bales of burlap sacks, some weighing up to eighty pounds, very tough to handle.

We were well off the coast of Jamaica by daylight on a five-day trip home—if the Good Lord was willing. Late on the second day our hearts were bouncing off the deck: The horizon just below the Yucatan was lined with Navy ships. Now, I mean *giant* ships. Two rows of them about a mile apart and our course was set right down the middle of those two rows. We were all freaking out, knowing there was way too much pot on board to get rid of.

"Take it easy," the Captain said. "I was in the Navy. I believe they're playing war games."

"What?"

"We're going to stay right on course," the Captain replied.

As it was, we ran right up the middle of a dozen battleships playing war games, carrying our ten thousand pounds of pot on board.

That night, passing through the Yucatan, the horizon was lit up with shrimpers. We took it off the automatic pilot and had two-hour watches. We played dodge boat between the dragging shrimpers most of the night. After that we didn't see another boat for the rest of our trip. Not until our friend met us at our meeting point, a buoy in the southwest pass of Egmont just after dark on a date we had preset.

Mike and I jumped into our friend's boat and raced to Pass-A-Grille High & Dry Marina where our skiffs were loaded with gas and ready to go. We then stopped by another waiting friend who had his boat gassed and ready to go along with parts and any extra fuel we might need. The four of us in our boats headed out Pass-A-Grille pass toward the southwest pass of Egmont to unload where we met Mammal and the Captain waiting just outside the buoy. It was about ten-thirty when we started unloading and well past midnight by the time we were done. Each boat, when unloaded, waited for the next to be loaded. We needed the help from everyone. It was a hell of an affair, a lot more work than we had planned it to be.

When all four boats were loaded, we headed to Sawyer Key and the place we'd cleared earlier for the unload. The tide was high and there was no problem entering at high water, but the tide had turned. It was going out. Mike and I had twenty-five-foot Lafitte Skiffs that drew three feet of water. We had two mullet boats with us. They were shallow-draft boats and drew almost nothing. We carried over three thousand pounds on the skiffs and the mullet boats carried between fifteen hundred and two thousand pounds. We had mountains of bales stacked on all the boats.

We worked the mullet boats close to the island where we could off-load and put them in the cleared spot with no problem at all. After the mullet boats were unloaded, it was my turn.

I headed my boat in toward the island and started bumping bottom. I got as close as I could without running high and dry aground. We had to carry bales on our shoulders in calf-deep mud, and it was quite a back-breaking situation. Once we finally got my boat unloaded, I backed off and started bumping again. I tried dredging my way to another deep-water canal at the north point of Sawyer Key where I finally ran aground.

My boat was so stuck in the mud that I could no longer move. I jumped out and headed back to Mike's boat. We had to unload his in deeper water off the edge of the canal so he wouldn't run aground like I did.

We carried the bales almost fifty yards. Mike, the boar hog, carried two bales at a time.

"Keep pushing on!" he yelled at the rest of us. "It'll be daybreak soon.

"Lamb! Get that bale out of the water! You weak-ass. Pick it up and put it on your shoulder."

We muled those bales through mud and knee-deep water until the sun rose. As it did, we covered our hill of bales with tarps to keep dry until we could return and again load our boats and take the pot to waiting vehicles at Tierra Verde, less than half a mile away.

As we headed back to the marina, we saw my poor boat lying high and dry on its side on the flats. The floorboards were covered with marijuana debris and it was completely out of the water.

"Get your ass back here in the morning at high water," Mike yelled, "and clean that boat up and get it ready for tonight."

117

"It'll be ready. Take it easy."

I caught a ride back to my boat with my friend in his mullet boat, and as we passed two local brothers, Baby Ray and Big Bill, friends of mine who were mullet fishing, they smiled when they saw me heading toward my boat.

"You must have caught a load of fish last night," shouted Bill with a big grin on his face. "Glad to see you got 'em on ice."

"Yeah. Wouldn't want them to rot."

They knew what time it was in the reefer business.

I retrieved my boat, cleaned it, fueled it and went home for some real sleep, just to arise before dark to go move bales again.

At sunset we met with our buyers, showed them where to put their vehicles. We had three groups, so we set up three different spots on Tierra Verde with three different times to meet (the buyers weren't eager to know one another and we thought it was important to keep them separate, too).

Mike and I used only our skiffs, not the little mullet boats, but we brought the mullet boat owners to help us load and unload. That way they'd surely earn the money we intended to pay them for last night and tonight. We pulled the boats up to the edge of the mangroves and jumped out. We grabbed the tarps and pulled them off.

"What the hell's going on here?" Mammal shouted. "Have you guys already loaded somebody?"

"No, why?"

"Fuck, Lamb, we had bales stacked over to that bush. There's about a ton missing."

"Damn right there's pot missing," Mike said. "We didn't have these bales stacked like this. This isn't even like we left 'em."

"Hey, those guys are on the seawall waiting," our other friend said. "This ain't the time to be worrying about some bales that we probably didn't even lose. Let's get loaded and get the hell out of here."

We loaded Mike's boat with what we figured was about thirty-five hundred pounds. He and the other guy left to meet the first group. They returned empty from the first unload, before Mammal and I loaded my skiff for the second group.

"What the fuck's going on?" Mike said. "You guys haven't done shit! What you been doing? Sleeping? Get your ass over to Hurricane Hole."

"Slow down and take it easy for a second. There's a boat on the other side of the island," I explained. "It's been running back and for—"

"Shut up! Let me hear it. Dry exhaust or wet?"

"What the fuck are you talking about?"

"I want to hear the exhaust and see if it's Bobby Summers. He shrimps almost every night. The last thing we need now is a Pinellas County sheriff." He listened. "It's dry. It's Bobby!"

I pulled into a mosquito ditch with a boatload stacked six feet high. He passed right by.

WE CLEARED OVER a million and a half dollars to split between a handful of friends. It would have been more if one of the guys hadn't ripped off those fifteen hundred pounds. (We figured karma would take care of the 'friend,' and it did, some years later.)

I now had a five-ton trip under my belt, and in spite of that one rip-off, the business was getting sweeter by the trip. Lots of beach families agreed; with every gig, an overflow of happiness and joy landed in their laps.

NINE

THE REEFER BUSINESS was snowballing. As sellers made more money, so did smugglers. It just brought more money into the game, as well as players. Vehicles, boats and tools for the trade became newer and more sophisticated. More opportunities came into our lives. We were offered stash houses, trucks, drivers, business fronts, investors and other groups of people who had boats, crews and the money to buy and do a load. But they didn't have the inside information nor the contacts.

When we discussed our next trip with the captain of the *Queen Angel,* greed got the best of him. He wanted a million dollars. *A million?* That was over half the profit.

"You'll never make the kind of money we paid you be-fore," I said, "even if you fill her belly full of snapper and grouper. You've bumped your head if you think anyone's paying you a million dollars to run a load."

So we went to Fort Myers and Captain Bob, a snapper fish-

erman with his own boat, the *Tiger Shark II*, a 65-foot Cyrus hull. He also had one hell of a dog, Lurch, a German Shepherd, who was better on a boat than most mates.

Bob had no problem with the money we offered.

"We'll be back in ten days ready to go," I told him. "And you'll be towing down one of our skiffs to use as a load and unload boat in Jamaica and back at St. Pete."

"Sounds good."

"Here's five grand. Fill a half a bin with ice, get plenty of food for five, any supplies you think we need, and top her off."

"Consider it done," he replied. "Lurch and I'll be waitin' on you guys."

Mike and I flew down to Jamaica, each of us carrying twenty-five thousand in hundred dollar bills. I also had crammed in my boots about a quarter pound of top-grade Indica seeds, in baggies. The Jamaican pot I was seeing in the fields was a Sativa strain, but I had something else in mind.

We gave the fifty thousand to Boobs as a down payment, and would have an additional hundred and fifty thousand on the boat when we got there. The seeds I'd take care of later.

This time we stayed at the Salem Beach Hotel, which was closer to St. Ann's Bay and Boobs' place. I was going to spend a few days in the fields. I wanted to teach the farmers some ways to grow a better product. The Indica plant produces a shorter, stouter, and fatter bud—and stronger smoke—than the long, stringier plants and buds of the Sativa strain, common of the Jamaican ganja.

On the last trip the boat was full of new tools they could use in the field. Now I wanted them to learn a new trick of the trade.

I saw a problem in the herb fields. Most farmers were throwing seeds in the ground and sexing them only *after* they flowered. That was too late to remove the "mad one," the male plant. They knew that the mad one would spoil the production of fine smoke by adding seeds to the buds on the female plants. I was tired of loads of weeds and seeds. The secret to good pot is pulling the males *before* flowering, which many farmers didn't know.

I explained to them that the trick is to keep the bud on the female horny; that she must yearn for sex. It is a seed-bearing weed and will produce offspring next year no matter what we do. But if we can control all the males, some of the females will 'queer off,' will turn to hermaphrodites, to sex a few of the other females and continue on with the seed line.

That as the buds grow, the hairs that turn red are the pistils. If the mad ones flower and pollinate the pistils, each pistil will turn into a seed, and produce no more THC.

"We want Sensimilla buds without seed, full of red hairs and no seeds," I said. "She will be producing THC 'til she gets sex. If we do not sex her, we will reap buds of THC until she dies. You understand?"

They always nodded, intent on learning more, though some of them preferred having the weight of seedy buds because that added to their profit.

"When yearning for sex, she'll get fatter, bigger and stickier. The bud gets fatter and stickier to catch the pollen in the air. If we kill the mad ones when they sprout, we'll have fields of much bigger and better smoke."

I walked through valleys and on mountaintops and it was all reefer, growing like corn in the Midwest. Walking up and down cliffs, walls and ledges of hills with the farmers, I had to stop and gulp for air many times. This Lamb was sure no mountain goat. I'd try to catch my wind while following little old farmers—who had to be a hundred years plus—who ran up and down the hills with ease. They were in the best shape I'd ever seen. Nonstop, they walked up and down hills all day.

For five days I taught the farmers about sexing the male plants before they flowered. Now it was time to go home.

We put together a fine load. This time I kept an eye on the size of the bales since on the last trip I had many bales weighing up to eighty pounds. Hell, we had one sleeping bag packed to the top that had to weigh at least 300 pounds. It was like carrying a coffin around. As such, it took four pallbearers just to get it on and off the boat.

But not this time. The whole ten thousand pounds was all thirty to fifty-pound bales, which completely filled a bedroom at Boobs' house to the ceiling. I told Boobs we'd return to our buoy in the bay in two weeks.

Mike and I flew back home, loaded Mike's skiff and headed for Fort Myers to meet Bob and his *Tiger Shark*. And his dog, Lurch.

On this trip we had a five-man, one-dog crew: Mike and myself, Big John, Strings, and Bob, the captain. We loaded supplies and crew and headed out of Fort Myers toward Jamaica.

"Watch the wheel, Lurch," Bob said, and the German Shepherd jumped up in the captain's chair, put his front legs on the big wooden star wheel and held course, (although we had it on automatic pilot). He did all his bathroom duties on the bow post, treating it just like a tree. A true sea dog, he lived on the *Tiger Shark* and kept his eye on that boat. That boat was his.

We passed the Dry Tortugas on the slow boat (it ran about ten knots) and when we hit the Yucatan Peninsula, it was night. Lights spotted the horizon. It was full of shrimpers. We took off the automatic pilot, moved Lurch from his perch, and took two-hour shifts dodging the lights. As we turned the west end of Cuba, we hit overhead seas.

It was only for one day but I loved that day. In spite of Lurch's use of the bow post, I sat right on it and the anchor rope, surfing the giant swells, taking a saltwater bath each time one came over the bow, enjoying being young and dumb. On the fifth day about two days off Jamaica's north coast, we started taking on water.

Strings and I were living in the bilge.

The packing in the shaft log came out. The whole shaft log was like a sprinkler. Our bilge pumps couldn't stay up with the incoming water. Mike and Bob, the boat's owner, called the trip off. No way we could put ten thousand pounds on with this kind of leak so we turned her around.

One night when the seas picked back up, Mike's skiff was taking a beating off the stern of the Tiger Shark. It was late in the night and rough. Thank God Captain Bob was on watch. He knew every sound of his boat. The three-quarter-inch nylon anchor rope towing the twenty-five foot skiff broke. Bob heard the snap. He backed down on the boat and hit the lights.

"Everyone get your ass up and on deck," he yelled, waking everyone up.

"What happened?" Mike yelled.

"The rope broke towing your boat. Lamb, get up here and get the spotlight," he ordered as he turned the boat around. "Start swinging that light!"

I ran to the bow and straddled the bow post. A good five to six foot swell was coming straight out of the north. Strings and Mike were on each side of the wheelhouse.

"All I see is swells and whitewater."

"Lamb, get your ass on the roof!" Mike yelled. "We gotta find my boat."

"How far back did we lose it? I was sound asleep."

"We all were. Bob was the only one on watch."

"I don't see shit up here."

We looked for the Lafitte Skiff. It was gone. We searched for over fifteen minutes and there was no sign of her. The ocean was nasty and all I saw was whitecaps. "Fuck, there's nothing out there. Where the hell did we lose it at, Bob?"

"It should be right around this area. I heard it the second we lost her. Keep your eyes open, boys. We'll find 'er."

I wasn't so sure; this will suck if Mike loses his boat.

In the pitch-black darkness, the turbulence of the phosphorescence from the waves and bubbles lit up the water. We finally spotted the skiff, floating and lost. The sea looked alive with movement and who knew whatever creatures were out there in those streaks of phosphorous. Every so often the skiff came back into view. Someone had to go overboard and swim to the boat and climb up into her. We drew straws.

Strings pulled the short one.

He had to dive into the middle of the dark, black nightmare out in the middle of the Yucatan off the Cuban coast with no land in sight. In fact, most of the time there was nothing in sight; we could hardly keep our eyes on the skiff although it was right next to us. Once in those seven-foot swells from hell, we could lose Strings. And there was a four-knot current.

But when he dove over, it looked like he was walking on water. Like he grew wings. He didn't even climb into the skiff. He jumped in it and brought it close enough for us to toss him a tow rope. We tied the skiff off and pulled it so Strings could jump into the big boat between swells. He saved the day, or should I say, saved the Knight. We hooked the boat up, tied it off, and started towing it north. Strings had balls. He easily could have been lost. He was definitely one of the best crew members in the business.

The next morning we had rounded Cuba and were off Dry Tortugas. Everyone was eager to get home. The conditions were excellent for the twenty-five-foot skiff to run in. Swells in the Gulf were one to two feet. Perfect for the Lafitte. Mike, Strings and Big John took off in the skiff just north of Dry Tortugas. They would be heading home at 35 to 40 miles an hour. They'd be taking a fresh water shower by nightfall.

"We'll see you later," they said, leaving Bob and me to run for another day and a half at seven to eight knots maximum, back to Fort Myers.

I got back to Fort Myers and had to be brought back to the burg by a pickup truck. I got fucked on that deal, but thank God we got the *Tiger Shark* home in one piece. Chalk that one up to experience.

TEN

"YOU KNOW, MIKE, we need to go into brokering the pot. We don't need to go down on any more boats ourselves."

"You don't have to tell me that. I've already got someone's boat and crew in mind."

"What're we going to do about the ten thousand in the bedroom in Boobs' house? I sure as hell don't want to ride another slow-ass boat back down when we can fly down, load the boat and fly back and have a week to wait on 'em."

"Hell, yeah. That's exactly what we're gonna do."

"Between our skiffs we can handle a little over seven thousand pounds. We can hire a couple of other boats to help us unload at the southwest pass."

"You're reading my mind, Lamb."

We each had close friends we trusted and hung out with who were excellent with boats and great on the water and ready to make a chunk of money.

A lot of college guys from Gainesville, friends of the schooling guys, Hub and Big Jim from the beach, started hanging out at the Pier and getting involved in the trade. Big Jim's friend, Kelly, and Kelly's brother, Miguelito, had a landscaping business on a spread of land up there they called the Ponderosa. The property had a big, high hurricane fence plus a couple of big, red Dobermans. And one hell of a party house. It was a great place for stashing herb and trucks.

We started finding our own boats and crews, but Mike and I still worked together hand in hand. It was much easier and more organized if we sent a boat down with a crew. We'd then fly to Jamaica and see Boobs. We would give him a few weeks' notice on how much weight we'd need at the beach house, the date of arrival, and just how much money was coming down to pay for the pot.

Plus we'd be in Jamaica to keep an eye on things. We'd meet the boat at the St. Ann's buoy marker on our preset date.

Most important, we'd make sure the bales were filled with fresh buds, look for the best burlap sacks so the bales didn't fall apart, and, for the first time, take a count of how many bales went on the boat.

It made for one hell of an exciting tropical vacation. We'd load the boat, see it off, then fly home and have our skiffs and transports ready for the off-load at our meeting marker in the southwest pass of Egmont. We had radio handles preset for contact. Sometimes we met just outside Pass-A-Grille Pass, closer to Tierra Verde, the most desolate, and therefore, most desirable place to unload contraband.

And unloading the boat into the trucks was done the same night, with the trucks on the road and gone within hours of arrival of the boat. Not like those trips where we unloaded, stashed the pot in the swamps, then went and set up our transports, came back, loaded our boats and then had to load the trucks and have them on the way. This was mo' better by far.

We worked through the next fall and summer crops, and Mike and I were like windshield wipers, back and forth from Jamaica to Florida. We did a handful of trips with other groups of our friends and their boats—sailboats or small commercial grouper and snapper boats. We were doing a load every month or two.

The sailboats didn't hold much with all the luxuries of home inside and they were slower than a boat pushed with a constant diesel engine. A boat under power, you could pretty much bet on the time of arrival, but the sailboats could run into stale air, with not a breath of wind. And when they were under power, their speed was half of that of a powerboat. Nevertheless, you could count on a sailboat always coming home. It didn't run out of fuel. If it didn't have wind today, it probably would tomorrow. One way or the other it would return to home port.

The trips we were doing were small, mostly two- to four-ton trips, sometimes up to ten thousand pounds apiece. Money was being made, but the split was so many ways, with other peoples' boats and crews (including Mike's)—plus they often wanted to sell their own pot—that it really cut into my share. Their rationale was that as long as they had to provide boats, crews, fuel and supplies, as well as take most of the risk, and all we were doing was loading and unloading, they deserved a larger share. *They forgot we had the contact.*

I finally had enough 'tropical vacations' to realize I should be in it for the money, like Mike was—"Hey, Weevil, are you ever gonna quit being a people pleaser and get the share you ought to? Shit, you're becoming half Jamaican, plus you're the one taking the risk unloading the big boat." He was right. It was time for me to play ball.

ELEVEN

IF I WAS going to play ball on a team to make *real* money, I had to own the team. I also had to own the ballpark, and the balls. Even all the concessions.

That way I could take great care of Boobs on the south end and my crew in the middle running the pot up to me. And then give my people on the north end, the buyers, a good price.

Most of my hits had been singles. If I was going to step into the batter's box, with the bases loaded, I had to hit a grand slam and put some points on the scoreboard.

By this time I was involved in tons and millions of dollars in the trips I'd done and still wasn't a millionaire, although Mike had hit the golden mark a few times.

"You want to go with Strings and me on his boat to Freeport?" Mike asked me one day. "I'm taking seven hundred grand to put in the bank."

I thought a minute: Strings had a Donzi that ran sixty miles an hour. We could be over there in an hour and a half. "Hell, yeah. I'd love to go. What about Mammal? Can we bring him along?"

"Sure. He's cool. John Carroll's going to meet us there, too."

John Carroll, the original Zorro, was a close friend of ours and loved us like sons.

So the four of us trailered this nineteen-foot flat-bottom lake boat over to Strings' sister's house in Stuart. There we spent most of the night counting the seven hundred thousand, piling the bills in five thousand dollar stacks before putting them in an army duffel bag. We headed out the next morning.

Mike and I sat in the rear seat, with the duffel bag between us on the floor. In front of us, Mammal and Strings sat in pedestal seats that freely turned 360 degrees. By now we were in the Gulf Stream and waves were breaking in the middle of the boat.

"Strings, slow the damn boat down," I hollered. "It'll come apart at this speed. Look at this set wave right in front of us!"

WHAM! A huge wave hit Mammal in the middle of his chest and spun his chair around. He fell flat on the deck along with thirty gallons of water.

"Shit, turn this boat around," I yelled. "We're gonna sink!"

Mammal tried to return to his seat but ended up in my lap when the next wave hit.

"Strings, there's two foot of water in the fuckin' boat," Mike shouted. "Mammal, grab hold of my duffel bag. Slow this fucking thing down, Strings! It's gonna stall!"

"Stall, my ass," Mammal yelled. "It's gonna sink!"

I shoved him. "Get off my lap, Mammal, and grab the money."

"HOLD ONTO THE MONEY!" Mike bellowed. Another wave. The engine stalled.

"Get the engine cover up!" Strings yelled.

Mike was already on it and had the cover up. He was half over the back seat and had hold of the bilge pump.

There was no float! "Turn on the pump, Strings!"

It was his boat; he'd already pulled the switch and water was shooting out the backside. I was next to Mike in deep prayer. Mammal was holding onto a very wet duffel bag. And Strings was struggling to start the engine, which finally came alive.

Mom's always saying God has a purpose for me, but at times like this, I figure it's just to scare the shit out of me.

We were so close to sinking I don't know how we got the engine started and floundered our way back into the Stuart inlet, to the marina, where we tied up. Shit! We didn't make it two miles out.

Mike opened his duffel bag and grabbed two handfuls of wet stacks of money. He handed them to Strings. "Trade this fuckin' flat bottom ski boat in and get a real boat that'll make it to the Bahamas!"

Luckily the marina had a showroom. Strings bought a  twenty-six foot Trojan, inboard, big-block, 454 Merc Cruiser, center console with bathroom, high free board, and was really a very nice boat.

The next morning we tried again and off to the Bahamas we went.

The Trojan was a much more capable boat to cross the Gulf Stream. It wasn't going to sink.

But we had no electronics.

We did, however, have a built-in compass.

As we entered the Gulf Stream this time, it was firing. The Gulf Stream runs four knots to the north. When the wind blows out of the north straight into the current, the waves jump like flames—it *fires*.

I sat with my back against the engine box watching the turquoise prop wash jumping five and six feet into the air, up and down and drifting into deep, dark blue ocean swells. We planned on making the trip in three hours.

Three hours came and went. I was still watching prop wash dancing behind the stern with no land in sight. Four hours passed, then five, then *six.*

"Strings! You see any land up there?" I asked. "It's only sixty-five miles. We should've been there a couple hours ago."

"Nope. Not yet. Something's got to be coming up soon, though."

Another hour passed. Mammal was hanging on the starboard side of the center console, Mike on the port. Strings had hold of the wheel in the center. It was so rough, no one had moved for hours. At least I was sitting down with my back against the engine box. The first six or seven hours I didn't see the sun until it was overhead. Now it was beginning to set in front of me.

As the eighth hour approached, we all began to wonder if we had missed the Bahamian chain.

Strings backed down on the big 454 and brought her to an idle. Mike pulled out the chart we had bought at the marina and we looked at it again for the second time today.

"Well, we're running on course," he said. "We've got about a four-knot tide running to the north."

"Yeah, right, Mike," I said. "It's still dark, deep water and we haven't seen anything that looks like shallow water. Or any land on the horizon. We might've missed the fuckin' Bahamas!"

"Shut up, Lamb," Strings shouted. "We're not running as fast as we planned. It's a lot rougher out here than I figured on."

"Yeah, right, Strings. We've been running eight friggin' hours. We'll be hitting Europe pretty soon."

"What the fuck are you talking about?"

"We probably missed the Bahamas."

Mammal didn't say a word, standing motionless like a statue.

"Take it easy, guys," Mike said. "We've been on course. We'll be seeing some land soon."

"I hope so," I said. "I'm so sunburned I feel like a piece of leather."

"Yeah, Lamb," Strings chimed in. "You look like a lobster."

"I'll throw your skinny ass over and see how you swim, Strings. Let's get this boat going."

The sun was much lower on the horizon now and nightfall would be in a couple more hours. This could be one hell of a fuckup.

A few minutes later, Mike looked up at the sky. "See those clouds over there and those colors? There's land under those clouds. Change course a little."

"Shit, Mike. We're five hours overdue," I complained. "We probably missed the island as it is. We don't know where the hell we're at."

"Just change course to those clouds."

Forty-five minutes later, land ahoy. Damn if he wasn't right. We finally docked to clear Customs.

Our three-hour trip had taken us nine.

We were sunburned, wind-blown and looked like salted strips of beef.

Mammal's waist-length hair stuck straight out in all directions as if he'd stuck his hand in a light socket.

Muscle-bound Knight, darker than the Bahamian officers themselves, with his straight, long Indian hair with a headband holding it down, and Strings with his Albert Einstein look, and then me with my lobster-red body plus my wild-ass Phyllis Diller do, captivated the Immigration officers. They could not take their eyes off us. They must have felt like they were the SPCA taking in a bunch of abandoned puppies. We had no problem clearing Customs.

As soon as Mike hit the dock with his duffel bag, he was gone to visit John Carroll. I told him before he left that we'd have a room waiting at the Beach Marina Hotel. We didn't see him for at least seven hours. When he returned, he was all smiles. "All business is taken care of," he said, "and I got us reservations for a flight leaving in the morning."

Hell, with that nightmare of a nine-hour boat-beating, sunburning, salt-sprayed crossing we took, we were all on that bandwagon. Hell, *yeah!* We'd much rather fly across the Gulf Stream drinking margaritas and piña coladas, laid back in a nice, comfortable, air-conditioned jet watching fine stewardesses serve us peanuts and drinks as they wriggled up and down the aisles.

But Strings did have a new boat, worth much more than the Donzi, and he owned it now and it was his. So Mike told him he'd have to find his way home alone.

"Florida's due west," Mike said.

TWELVE

SO MIKE AND I stayed ping-ponging from Pass-A-Grille to Jamaica, loading and unloading our boats and the boats of our friends. One day Big Jim and his Gainesville friend, Kelly, called me. They wanted me to load their gem of a boat, a 1939 gaff rig twin-masted schooner, seventy feet long, built by Alden Boat Works.

I went up to Gainesville and agreed to organize a trip. I set up where and when to load, and where and when to off-load at Egmont. We were going to meet in the south-west pass.

The schooner was in Key West. I took Strings and a couple of the Gainesville crew down there.

I put Dwayne—Pa—and Prairie Dog on board with Strings and Miguelito. When Pa was in St. Petersburg, I took him stone crabbing. He could pull a sixty-pound wooden triangle stone crab trap faster than my winch for the better part of a day. A solid muscle of a man.

But Strings was the man I put in charge.

The load was not at the beach house this time. The Jamaicans were working on the road and had it all torn up down to the beach house, so we loaded at Flat Point, another little spot near Salem Beach. I met the big, black twin-masted ghostly looking schooner just off the bay. She was filled with clothes, shoes and tools for the Jamaicans. I took her in closer to the beach where we waited for the herb to come down in sugar cane trucks. It was a nice white sandy beach, but there was a reef just outside that was razor sharp and bone dry.

I attached glow lights to crab buoys and broke them just below the water line to mark off a little cut in the reef where my small boat could run. The lights lit it up nicely.

Cyrus, police chief from St. Ann's, had been sent by Boobs to make sure everything went right. He wanted to be sure the cane trucks would have no problem coming down to the shoreline from Murray Mountain, passing through Alexandria and Brownstown to their destination on the beach.

When the trucks showed up and stopped, they looked alive with people. Children, scrawny young men, and little old men, hiding up under the frames of the trucks, hiding just to be able to make some tip money by helping to load. They came running out of the trucks like ants to sugar.

"Grab him, mon. Grab him," Cyrus yelled out.

Three black guys raced after and captured a young black man. Cyrus smacked the dude across the head with a sugar cane stalk. "Him be snitch to the police. Him is rat, mon. Him tell of this herb business tonight."

Cyrus had the snitch by his hair and was beating the shit out of him. The police informant was bleeding badly.

Cyrus dragged him over to me. "Steve, you take him, mon. Take him out to the big boat. Get rid of him on your way back. Throw him over. Him as big a snitch in Jamaica. Him tell the police what happening, brother."

"There's no way he will be hurt anymore," I told Cyrus. I set the guy down by a fallen coconut tree with three of Boobs' men and told them to make him smoke until long after the boat had left. I kept checking the badly beaten snitch and they kept the chalice (a half a coconut used as a pipe) filled. It held over an ounce of pot at a time. There was no way I was going to have a killing involved on my trip.

After loading the last load, I gave hugs and high-fives to Strings and the rest of the crew and then let the Jamaicans break into the mountain of gifts—shirts, pants, shoes and tools. There were little kids with two left shoes on their feet. Guys with a size 12 on one foot and a size 10 on the other. Kids with shirts so big they looked like pajamas. But they were in heaven. It was all white teeth and smiles. Seeing these men with real Levi's on made their day and mine, too. Half of them didn't own a pair of shoes. Some had never had shoes on. Some had feet as wide and as calloused as an elephant's hoof and their feet wouldn't fit in a pair of shoes. As I sent the boat on, I made sure all gifts were distributed equally, talked with Cyrus and went and checked on our snitch. He continued to smoke, and the three of Boobs' men sat with him until well after daybreak. That dude was so stoned he couldn't move.

The Wanderlust was taking home seven thousand pounds, and she was stuffed. For a seventy-foot schooner, she had no room in her at all. Strings and Dwayne had to tear out the forward room just to get the seven thousand in her.

It would be eight days until I saw the *Wanderlust* again. I had prearranged with Strings to meet her at the southwest pass Egmont at a bell buoy.

As I've said before, Strings was one of the best captains around. You could count on him to bring the load home. If something broke he was the one to fix it and if it couldn't be fixed, he'd come up with something to substitute for the problem. We'd done a lot of shark fishing around the buoy where I'd be waiting on him. But this time he wasn't there.

Just after dark on the eighth night, Little Jimmy, my helper and I were set up off the meeting marker. Big Jim was with us in his boat. I called on the radio with no reply. I tried over and over. *They should have been here hours ago. What could have happened?*

"I don't know what's going on, Big Jim," I said around daybreak. "You head home and get some sleep. I'll call you later, around four." He left, and Little Jimmy and I sat at the bell buoy until well after sun up. Finally we gave up and headed back to Strings' house to get some sleep.

"We'll try again tonight," I said.

We tied up next to Strings' boat. As soon as we hit the bed we were out. It felt like I'd only been to sleep an hour or so when the next thing I knew, Strings was shaking me.

"Get the fuck up, Lamb! What are you doing sleeping in my bed? You were supposed to unload me last night."

"What the fuck happened, Strings?"

"Shit, man. Those guys are scared to death to get near shore. I went over the charts to show them what buoy we were supposed to be at, where you wanted us. But they're sitting twenty miles offshore."

"I called you the entire fuckin' night, Strings. I've only got ten-twelve miles range on my handheld. You know that. What the hell you mean they were scared to come into shore? The bell buoy's no where near shore. How'd you get in here, Strings?"

"Took the thirteen-foot Boston Whaler. They'll be in after dark."

"Shit, I hope so. I waited until after sunrise this morning. Let's take your Trojan, Strings. And my boat. We'll top 'em off at the marina, then I'll go and talk to the buyers and have the Winnebagos and trucks set up on the point inside the Tierra Verde bridge and the other group at Hurricane Hole. With both boats we can handle the whole seven thousand pounds."

"Let's go and top things off and I've got to come back and get a little sleep."

"Yeah. Let Little Jimmy crash here, too. He needs some sleep for tonight so he can toss some bales. I'll tell Maslanka to be at the marina just before sunset and we'll head out."

We headed out Pass-A-Grille Pass and turned south for Egmont. Big Jim (Paper Ass) was with me, and so was Little Jimmy (Sunshine). Strings was right along beside me in his twenty-six-foot Trojan, which he had broken in well coming back from the Bahamas alone.

There we were, well after dark again, and no answer. Again. About ten thirty I saw a little flicker of light just about a mile south of the buoy and I thought it was strange. So I eased over and a mile off the southwest buoy, I could see a dark black outline of a vessel. When I cruised up on it, there was the *Wanderlust,* just floating along. No one out on deck. I pulled up beside it. "What's up?" I yelled out.

The crew sprung out on deck and looked back at us.

"Where the hell you guys been?" I asked.

"Oh, we've been playing cards."

"Cards? What the fuck? You guys are floating around out here with almost two million dollars' worth of weed onboard? Let's get this show on the road."

I called Strings who was still sitting at the buoy and told him to come over to the blink of light. He eased on over. The crew started tossing bales onto my boat. Strings tied up on the other side and started loading bales on to his boat, too.

Big Jim and I were stacking bales as tight and as efficiently as possible. I had my skiff three-quarters of the way full when I noticed water coming in from the floorboards. I started shifting bales around to find that my rear floorboard had broken under the weight of the bales.

I lifted up the board, and saw that my four-inch exhaust had broken out of the stern.

I was taking on water fast. So I shifted bales and started my boat. Just then a bright light hit me square in the face. "What the fuck?" I yelled.

"Tugboat to the west!" Dwayne answered. "It's just swinging its light looking for channel markers."

"Hell, it came right across me and the bales."

"C'mon, get your boat back over here. Get these bales off."

"Take it fuckin' easy. It's sinking. Can't put on any more bales. Got to run this water out. Be back in a sec."

But once I had the bilge dry and the exhaust put back into place, it was still leaking. How the hell was I going to get any more bales on board. I'd have to keep moving. I kept running in circles around the *Wanderlust* like Indians around a wagon train. I loaded the last quarter load of my boat cruising past the *Wanderlust* and Strings' boat while they shot-put bales on my skiff, all the while being lit up by a tugboat who must have wondered why I was running around in circles.

When I had a five-foot stack, Big Jim and I headed for Tierra Verde, Hurricane Hole, passing Egmont on the inside. The beam from the lighthouse lit up our load every thirty seconds.

"Damn, Lamb. This lighthouse is driving me nuts. Reminds me of a prison break."

I laughed at the thought.

"Not funny, Lamb. I hope this isn't some kind of an omen."

That omen lifted as we finally got out of the light's range and closer to the unload where there was a nice, soft white beach I could run my boat up on. I had a sand shoe to protect my prop and shaft. Once high and dry on the sandy beach we filled a waiting Winnebago and a pickup truck that had a camper on its back, full of the

144

much-wanted herb. With my boat dry on the beach and all the weight from the bales off, I 5200'd my exhaust pipe back into place. Strings' boat, the high-sided Trojan, was so loaded with bales, they were higher than his head and as he eased in, he had a five-foot wake behind his boat. I'd never seen anything like this. It was so weighed down that the wake was even with his head as he steered. That Trojan was a mule.

The Hurricane Hole buyers were loaded and on the road. The next stop would be around the point on the east side of Tierra Verde bridge.

I finally got my leak stopped.

"Strings, I'll take your load with Little Jimmy over to the other side. You take my boat back, tie it up behind your house. I'll be there in an hour or two."

Jimmy and I headed toward the bridge. I stayed close along the seawall, wanting to stay out of sight. There were only two houses on all of Tierra Verde, Gramma Hubbard's house and Bobby Roberts's. This was a great place to unload.

As I approached the bridge with a three thousand-pound five-foot stack on which Little Jimmy was riding high, we plowed through a curtain of lead fishing sinkers attached to numerous fishing lines. I had run slap through the middle of four or five guys fishing for sheephead. They weren't happy.

"What the fuck do you think you're doing?"

"Damn! You just run over our lines!"

"Get the hell out in the pass where you belong!"

I still wonder today what those guys thought of what must have looked like a five-foot turtle shell cutting off their lines.

I slipped around the point behind the bridge to find my friends standing out on the seawall. Excitement was in their jumps and waving hands.

"Over here! Over here! We're over here!"

"No shit, Sherlock. I seen you a quarter mile away. Get them vehicles backed up to the seawall. Let's get 'er done."

We finally had the vehicles on the road and we never lost a pound to rip-offs or to the law. I paid Strings double what he usually made on gigs. Like I said, Strings was a good man and well worth it.

THIRTEEN

MIKE AND I were flooded with people banging on our doors with offers. The excitement, adventure and lure of easy money had caught on nationwide. In the early '70s, times were great on the beaches. We were young, happy, healthy and wealthy. For the most part, people on the beaches were carefree, living life to its max. Every night was a gathering of friends. We'd plan to meet on beaches or sand fills or along the seawall on Eighth Avenue in Pass-A-Grille. And there were our local watering holes, like Eagans, Clancy's, Crown Lounge on Tyrone Boulevard, as well as a club owned by Sammy, the Back Street, on Madeira Beach.

After Back Street, Sammy opened another night-club on St. Pete Beach called the Gallery, and that was our main hangout. It was one block from my mother's house. Boy, was that nice, walking those sweet young ladies right through a little dirt path I had between my neighbor's house and across a vacant lot. Straight into my back bedroom to do a line or smoke a joint and indulge in some of the best sex ever performed between young people on this planet. We had keg parties on desolate sand fills that are now golf courses of Isla del Sol condominiums and the sand fills of Tierra Verde that are now filled with homes. Money flowed. Everyone had trucks and dirt bikes we'd race in drunken competition, ripping up the fills with chicks bouncing off the back of our bikes, hanging on to us for dear life.

We had boats that taxied groups of kids to Shell Island and other sand shoals along Pinellas County coastline.

Life was a real beach. Hell, growing up there was fishing, fucking and financing happiness. And that's how many of us kids on the beach lived. It was a great time, like no other.

Million-dollar gigs were structured while partying and pre-announced gatherings would form with bands playing, tanned-bodied girls in bikinis dancing in the sand while we drank beers and smoked joints and discussed boats, the sizes, how much they could hold and who was going to be the crew.

If you had making big money on your mind, you couldn't sit around dreaming about it. You had to get up and do it. As more and more people and opportunities came my way, I became one hundred percent involved in pot smuggling.

ONE NIGHT AT a party, Mike and I talked about getting involved with some Cortezians, friends of ours who lived in

Cortez, a small fishing village on the south side of Tampa Bay. When we were just kids, we started fishing with these guys who were among the best fishermen in the area. They'd grown up with fathers and grandfathers who had been commercial fishermen their entire lives. Junior, a friend of ours, had access to large fishing boats, and he arranged one for us. Mike and I would load in Jamaica; the three of us would unload with our boats just south of Tampa Bay.

Junior knew of a good stash place just east of the bridge in Long Boat Key Pass: a mangrove island behind Jewfish Key, with a deep mosquito ditch running right through the middle of it.

Mike and Junior had two crew members on the boat. I put my friend Miguelito, from Gainesville, with them, filled the boat with supplies, and sent them south to Jamaica. Mike and I flew down and put a down payment on ten thousand pounds. When the boat arrived, we loaded it with wood carvings, parrots and ten thousand pounds of top-grade herb. Most of it was Indica buds from the seeds I had taken down before and crossed with two Jamaican strains, lamb's breath and cotton. The farmers I worked with began calling our new strain lamb's *bread,* because some of the buds were as large as loaves of bread.

We had the big snapper boat filled in less than four hours. It was slick calm and this was by far the best load ever sent back from Jamaica. Ninety-five percent of the load was red-haired buds without seeds and no 'mad' ones.

We flew home and met the snapper boat off Anna Maria, just south of Egmont Key.

149

Mike and I brought two guys with us. In Mike's skiff was a college football player, who'd never done drugs and who planned on being a politician. With me was Mannie, our all-around emergency mechanic who worked at the High & Dry Marina. My boat was all open and a foot longer than Mike's or Junior's, so I carried a few extra bales.

We all headed into Long Boat Key Pass running hard right under the bridge and east of Jewfish Key, the main island filled with all the giant Australian pines. Sliding over the sand flats, crossing the Intracoastal and into our mosquito ditch, all three boats entered the cut and idled to our cleared-out spot on the high, dry land in the mangroves. We unloaded my boat first, stacking all the bales neatly. Once the boat was empty, Mannie insisted on leaving.

"Hey, guys. I'm outta here. I'm taking this fishing pole I brought with me and I'm waiting for you just on the other side of the Intracoastal. I don't wanna be anywhere around this mountain of herb. I have nothing to do with this. I'm just a mechanic."

"That's why you brought your fishing pole?"

"You got it, Lamb. I'm taking this boat and I'll be fishing. I'm not going to jail for marijuana."

"Yeah, right. Like they won't know the boat was used to bring in a load? There's debris all over the floorboards. As if something happens, they're not going to know you're involved?"

"Lamb, you can forget that. I'm taking your boat and you guys can meet me at the Intracoastal just outside the mosquito ditch."

"Seventy-five yards away? Are you nuts?"

"What's going on?" Mike whispered. "What the fuck's wrong with Mannie?"

"He doesn't want to get involved with the load."

"It's a little late, ain't it? He just unloaded the big boat. That doesn't make much sense."

But for the next three hours Mannie did wait, anchored out in the middle of the pass, until the other two boats were unloaded and we came out from the middle of the mangroves and met back up with him.

We had the ten thousand pounds stacked and tarped. Five nights later we would load a Winnebago with some of the herb at Longboat Key Beach, just north of the bridge on the east side of the road, right along the water's edge. During that five-day period I went back one afternoon to check on the pot and to get a bale to be picked up the same night. Mike and I needed to pay a bill and planned to pay it with a bale.

I drove my 360 Yamaha dirt bike over the Skyway Bridge down to Cortez back behind the Shell gas station and turned off Cortez Boulevard, then down a dirt road that led to a mosquito ditch. I parked my bike, swam across the ditch, and walked to a thick wall of mangroves where we had the mound of pot.

I was separating one bale from the pile when I heard voices. Two guys in a little kicker boat were fishing in the mosquito ditch and they passed within a few yards of me while I was pulling a single bale from the ten thousand pound mound. They finally exited the west side of the mangroves and I hurriedly carried the bale to the island's point, for easier access with Little Dave's boat that night. I swam back across the mosquito ditch to my dirt bike, to ride back over the Skyway Bridge to St. Pete Beach. All was right with the world. The bale was ready for Little Dave and the reefer was nice and dry and ready to be loaded.

That night I returned with Little Dave and his boat. From Pass-A-Grille to Longboat Key Pass, the wind was blowing hard out of the northwest and the seas were three to five feet. And we had to pass that friggin' Egmont Key spotlight again. We got our brains beat out but made it home with the one bale.

151

On the fifth night we loaded the Winnebago right off the coastal road that ran over the Longboat Key Bridge. I sat with my boat up on the little beach a hundred feet northeast of the bridge. Every time a vehicle passed by we stopped, ducked down and waited. We hoped the Winnebago looked like fishermen with a camper. As soon as a car passed on by, we were back at it like squirrels stashing nuts in a hollow tree. We had the Winnebago loaded with three thousand pounds and out of there in less than an hour.

I returned to the seven thousand pounds that remained to help the others load my boat and Mike's. We were carrying it to a house Mike and I had rented on the water, right next to the Buccaneer Yacht Club and Restaurant on Longboat Key.

We had those seven thousand pounds piled up on the dock and along the seawall in the backyard, and trucks were lined up in our driveway for the load. One of them, a big six-wheel U-Haul moving truck, smashed into the roof of our carport right next to the restaurant. It made such a racket that the customers at the Buccaneer thought it was a car crash. People looked out big picture windows at our eight-foot high pile of bales on the dock and in the back yard. We just continued running a line of human bale carriers across the lawn, loading the truck that had just taken down half the carport roof, as at least forty or fifty highfalutin' well-to-do folks looked on, not really knowing what was happening. Only in the early '70s could you unload thousands of pounds of pot with an audience watching without the first call to the law.

Once our beach party was over, we headed back to Cortez, passing the Coast Guard station, and tied up at Bayshore Fish House. We cleaned our boats and drank a few beers. We had another one under our belts.

FOURTEEN

AS POT-SMUGGLING TRIPS made it in, things got better for all. We began traveling. We went on sport fishing trips, and hunting trips, and trips to Vegas, where we partied with the prettiest working girls in Sin City. They got to know us so well and liked us so much—and no doubt our money—they'd pick us up at the airport. All we'd have to do is call and tell them we were coming in.

We flew out to Vegas and partied in groups of four or five of us at a time a couple of times a month.

Groups of locals from the beach would just get together and plan neat things to do. Everyone could afford neat plans. Whatever we came up with, we did. I hadn't yet turned twenty.

Twenty-five or thirty of us would get together and rent the *Florida Fisherman* from Wilson Hubbard and go offshore to the middle grounds for a couple of days fishing and gambling. There'd be groups of people with giant poker games. Hubbard, the owner and captain, would be right in the middle of the poker games. We'd bet on the largest fish caught. Giant jackpots. Everyone threw money in. We brought

guns out there for large sharks that were brought to the side of the boat and to show off our shooting skills. We enjoyed the money and were not afraid to spend it as often as we could.

One night Mike and I went to dinner at Gene's Lobster House, Stuart Causeway, on Madeira Beach. We had a few drinks over a turtle dinner when he came up with a plan.

"Let's buy our own boat," he said, "a real boat, a shrimper, that can hold the mother lode, and I'll put up the money. I'll spend fifty thousand. You go to Key West and make the deal and I'll pay for it and have it put in a corporate name . . . or a fake one."

"Who'll crew?"

"We've got Mammal and Strings. We'll put someone else on with them. We'll load it, unload it. We can sell it to our Michigan friends. Unload it out of town. No one will ever know."

"Sounds good, Mike. We gotta stop shittin' where we sleep."

"I've got an unload at Bubba Capo's up in the Big Bend, a place called Steinhatchee."

"That's right across from Gainesville. If it's gonna be a mother lode, we could sell some to the Gainesville crowd."

"Bubba's got the unload boats and a big fish scow. Holds over twenty thousand pounds of fish."

I was on that idea like a monkey on a banana tree.

Mike gave me twenty-five thousand in hundreds. Two days later I took Mammal with me and we flew down in a little twin-engine private plane we rented out of Albert Whitted Airport in St. Petersburg.

Once I closed the deal the boat would be taken to Tampa Bay. Singleton Shrimp Company in Tampa. There the boat's owner would receive the remaining twenty-five thousand and we'd take ownership of the new vessel.

We had a room at the Pier House on the end of the island. There was a nice beach for the eye, a topless beach right outside our room. Mammal and I had a hard time keeping our minds on a shrimp boat deal. Seventy-five percent of the rooms at the Pier House were filled with tanned ladies ready to party Key West style, and that was *butt* naked, in the water, on the beach, in their room or our room. Whatever we wanted.

We finally made it over to Stock Island where the shrimp boats were docked. The difference between Key West and Stock Island was like night and day.

The weather was supposed to turn bad in the morning and it did. The docks were stacked three boats deep. We checked around and were sent to different boats but nothing panned out.

All I could think of was the money lying around tied up to these docks. All the boats. If we could just get captains and crews to run them to Jamaica, I would transport the whole island. After three or four days of bird-dogging, and I mean, through some real pirates, drunks and howling critters, we finally found a guy who wanted to sell his boat. He had a seventy-two-foot Desco and it had a hell of a belly. It was an ice boat with a hold big enough to bring home half of Jamaica. The boat was in good condition, and had a lot of electronics. This thing was just what the doctor ordered. Glen, the captain and owner, wanted forty grand.

The boat was also the boat Boobs had been praying for. This baby could bring home thirty to thirty-five thousand pounds, no problem. Mammal and I hung out with Glen for two days shooting pool and drinking beer in a little conch bar across from his shrimp boat. We set up a trial run to shake out any bugs and to get to know the boat's innards.

She had a big Detroit for power and a nice generator. Four bunks plus one in the forward cabin—the captain's quarters—where the controls were. The galley had a stove, refrigerator and the eating table was as big as our dining room table in the house I was born in.

We did a trial run off the Florida Straits. The first night I cleared a try-net, a smaller net that you try to test the shrimp grounds to see whether you want to let out the bigger nets or not. When I opened the try-net, a stingray, a real hot-tail, a big one, a good ten pounder, fell from the net and its barb went right through my rubber boot and stuck in the front of my ankle, breaking off. Instant pain. My foot swelled to the size of a basketball. The worst pain I've ever been in. Glen had one red on board, a Seconal. And son, it was a lifesaver.

We immediately headed back to Key West and I crawled off the boat and was taken to the hospital where they cut the stingray's barb out of my ankle. I returned on crutches the next day to meet with Glen to close the deal. This boat was just what we needed. Mike would be happy when this gem arrived in Tampa.

We had a big, steaming bowl of shrimp for lunch at the bar, and Glen hit me with a punch of shocking news. "I can't sell this boat, Steve. It's my livelihood. If I sell her I'll have forty grand to my name and that's it. This boat feeds my family. I can't work as a deck hand on any other boats, not when I've worked all these years to own my own boat. I'm sorry, Steve. I've thought about it for the past two days. It's all I have. I really need the money. I need to sell it, but my family will eventually starve if I don't have my own boat."

Glen was a very smart man, plus he had twice the age on us. We were the long-haired kids and with enough cash to buy a boat that Glen had worked his whole life for.

I don't know what it was, but the shrimper that Glen owned was the dream of my life, and I dreamed to have her stuffed to the running boards.

"Glen, listen. You want to keep your boat and make the twenty-five thousand I have jammed in my boots?"

"Son, let's ease on over to the galley."

We walked across the street and climbed aboard his boat. "Well now," he said, "what exactly do the two of you have on your minds?"

"You ever hear of an island named Jamaica?"

He looked at me. "So?"

"Do you have a chart of the Yucatan and Jamaica?"

He reached over his head and pulled a chart out, one amongst many, and spread the chart. I pointed to the north coast.

"Glen, I'll pay you twenty-five thousand and you keep your boat. I want to go to the north coast of Jamaica and pick up a load of marijuana. Then return to a spot off the coast of Florida and unload it."

He squinted at me.

"You'll never touch land," I assured him. "Everything will be done offshore."

"How soon we going?"

He was in! "Well, Glen, I need about a week to get things ready." I reached down into my boot and pulled out some bills. "Here's ten thousand now for you and any bills you or your family have." I handed him the money, and continued. "Fill the boat up, take it to Tampa and be at Singleton Shrimp Company. Get any parts you need and I'll contact you there in a week. And this doesn't come off your bill. You're still getting paid twenty-five. This is for good show."

I was gone with a handshake and a heart full of trust. I read him as a good man.

I returned to St. Pete and went over things with Mike. We ran around buying much needed clothes, tools and food for the people in Jamaica. We also bought two twenty-one-foot naval Zodiac rafts that could be blown up with scuba tanks. Each raft would hold three thousand pounds. We would use these to load and again to unload off the coast of Florida.

We bought thousands of dollars' worth of gifts for the Jamaicans, supplies and anything needed on our trip.

Our crew would be Strings, Mammal and Glen.

A week later we were in Tampa with Glen and going over where and when, what date and what buoy in St. Ann's Bay off Jamaica to be in, and where to meet off the Big Bend of Florida, Steinhatchee. When, where and what dates.

We went over radio handles for contact when offshore. I was the Red Fox. Glen was Night Hawk. If there were any problems, he was to come back the same time the next night.

We loaded all our supplies on to the boat at Singleton's Shrimp House in Tampa. We also loaded Strings and Mammal, and the 72-foot fat-bellied shrimper slipped out of Tampa Bay headed toward Jamaica.

Mike and I were busy running around setting up times, dates and places for our trucks, drivers and buyers. The buyers, who actually owned the trucks, had to know where to put them and how long to keep them there. The problem was we had to synchronize times and places for 18-wheelers to park but not raise suspicion, and then get loaded and be able to hit the highway and be northbound with no problem.

We then had to meet with Bubba in the same area as the trucks would be to set up our unload with the little boats and the big fish scow that Bubba owned. There was a lot of organizing.

After all was set up with the unload and transport end to make sure everything was on time and in the right places, Mike and I had to fly to Jamaica. It took four days just to truck thirty thousand pounds to the stash house on the coast. A canoe was ready to take us out the night of the scheduled rendezvous and we'd use that along with the two Zodiacs to load the big boat off of St. Ann's buoy.

After the shrimper was loaded and on its way, Mike and I would fly back to Florida, drive up to Bubba's and do the unloading and make sure all the big trucks were filled and on the road all over again. We had our work cut out. We would be on nonstop go from sunup to sundown for the next two weeks.

When everything was set and ready in the United States, we flew to Jamaica, Mo Bay. Yeah, you guessed it: we checked into the Playboy Club and sexed out with the bunnies we'd met on past trips. It was always Easter in Ocho Rios. That club was full of some of the finest-looking bunnies in the world and we had their favorite friend.

He was an old, fat bald-headed man but the bunnies loved him. His name was Benjamin Franklin. Everybody loved him. The women, the hotels, the airlines, car rentals, clothes shops, wood carvers. Everyone liked Benjamin. And he was my big brother, Brother Ben. I liked him. In fact, I loved him. After three days of wining, dining and sexing at the Club, it was a good night's sleep and off for a few days of gathering herb.

We moved into the beach house. Every night one or two big sugar cane trucks showed up carrying six or seven thousand pounds in a load. As the loads came down, we stuffed the bedrooms completely to the ceiling. Once they were filled, we continued to fill the hallway and the bathroom as well. When we weren't busy unloading and stacking loads, we sat around talking with a half dozen of Boobs' men, telling tales of different lives and the way we'd grown up and the lives we'd lived. It was no wonder we became great friends. We slept on the living room floor and couch.

Each day seemed like a week while we were waiting, so many things passed through my mind.

What if I'm busted here in Jamaica, sleeping in this house with thirty thousand pounds of herb under my head? What if the boat breaks down on the way? What if everyone at home is not on standby? Will the trucks break down on the interstate? What'll it be like being a millionaire? I'd own ten thousand pounds of pot myself. I'd have over a million dollars when all was said and done. If God was willing.

The day we had waited so long for, finally dawned. By night we'd have the house full of Jamaicans—over two dozen big, strong workers to help load, while I called on my radio for Night Hawk.

More and more Jamaicans arrived. The house was loud with reggae music and a living room and back pool area filled with Jamaicans with long dread locks waiting to give us a helping hand. And to receive the long-awaited gifts that were on their way from the United States for them and their families.

Just before dark the transport canoe showed up. Mike and I had the radio and we eased offshore after dark. We were at the buoy for an hour or so.

"Red Fox to Night Hawk. Howaboutcha?"

No answer. Was all this going to be a nightmare or a dream come true?

Close to two hours of waiting, I heard a long awaited response.

"Yeah, how about you there, Red Fox. It's the Hawk. C'mon?"

"Yeah, Hawk. I gotcha. We're about ten miles out here headed your way. Come on."

"Yeah, we're on a KOA, standby."

About forty minutes later the purr of a diesel grew louder. The big, dark figure of a shrimper slipped toward us. We made contact and jumped on board. It was all hugs and smiles.

"Let's get it on," I yelled.

We moved in shore right off Boobs' house. No one in sight. The crew had the two twenty-one-foot naval rafts blown up and ready to put overboard. They had nine-horse outboards for power. We arranged the three load boats, the canoe and the two rafts. We loaded the two rafts with the gifts and supplies for our loyal friends on the beach. I also had Boobs' duffel bag of money.

At the coral reef wall, the Jamaicans had already piled up a mountain of herb. A long line of Jamaicans continued to bring bales from the house, like worker ants carrying food to their queen.

We stacked up the gifts and supplies to be given out later and began the bale-passing process.

We put a few Jamaicans on board, though most of them were frightened to get on a boat. Strictly land people, they'd never been *in* the water, let alone on a boat floating on top of it. Of the few who did go out to help us load the big boat, many got sick and we had to return them to land.

Things went well until the net in our raft, surrounding three thousand pounds, began to give way as it was being winched up.

"Mike, you got hold of your side of the net? My side's starting to rip . . . Mammal!—give us some slack on the lines holding this raft—the net's starting to rip—Mike, push the raft off the side of the boat! My side's starting to give way! *SHIT!* My side's stuck on the boat! Mammal, slow down on the winch! *STOP THE FUCKIN' WINCH, MAMMAL!*"

"Weevil, what the hell's going on over there?"

Before I could answer, bales began raining on us like giant hailstones. We were blanketed with bales and knocked into the water. I didn't know up from down or down from up; I just knew I was in the ocean. Once I fought my way up through the bales and broke surface and got some air into my lungs, I realized three thousand pounds were swimming with me.

"Mike! You all right?"

"Yeah, you?"

"I think so. I got the shit knocked out of me."

"What the hell happened, Lamb?"

"I told you the net was caught on the side of the boat and they kept running the winch and one of the corner rings ripped out. Next thing I knew it was raining bales. We lost that load."

"That's all right, there's plenty more on the beach." Mike climbed into the raft. "Let me give you a hand, Weevil."

He pulled me into the raft and I saw there were a few bales still there, but as I looked around, with the moon high in the sky, I saw the ocean was dotted with bales floating for as far as the moon's light allowed me to see.

We handed up the few bales that hadn't fallen overboard and then headed back to shore for more, continuing to fill up again and again.

Finally, the main hull was full.

We smiled and hugged and then began to load the boat again with all the head carvings and wood characters we'd acquired. We also sent out two parrots to take home. We wished the best to our crew and told them we'd be waiting for them at our destination at the spot in Florida in seven days.

"Yeah. We'll see you. God bless."

Mike and I flew back to the States and started setting up the work to be done for the unload: trucks, boats, people, places, dates and times. We stayed in a triplex in Indian Rocks where all three apartments were rented by members of our group—Mammal, Big Jim, and Bill, one of our Michigan buyers. We worked out of Mammal's place since he was on the boat.

As the seventh day came closer, we focused strictly on the unload. We would stash the load and then fill up the trucks the next day after we had weighed it. We wanted to get a weight and bale count for each transport.

We hired two other close friends, Barry and Rusty, to help us unload.

We drove north in two vehicles to Steinhatchee, headed toward Bubba's house to set up.

FIFTEEN

ONCE IN THE country of Bubba, it was like going back in time. He lived in a small house deep in the woods. In his back yard was a big pot for boiling and cleaning wild hogs he trapped and shot.

Bubba, like me, didn't have the best education, but he owned one of the largest fish houses in Steinhatchee and caught, by far, the most fish in the area. He was one of the best fishermen on the Gulf Coast, catching trout, redfish, mullet, and any other thing that swam.

We had most of our supplies but went to a little country store to fill up some gas jugs and pick up a few extra things to eat. We bought sardines and Happy Jack cookies, the only food on the otherwise empty shelves.

Just before we drove away, I told Mike we ought to try out the radio.

"This is the Red Fox calling Night Hawk, C'mon."

"Weevil, you nuts? We only have a fifteen mile—"

"A'yeah. This is Hawk. I gotcha Red Fox. C'mon."

"Lamb! You got a copy? He's on the radio."

"No shit. I'm talking to him."

"Hawk, we're putting the wood on the fire. We'll have the barbeque ready just after dark. We'll see you for dinner. Come on."

"A'yeah, we've got all meat and no potatoes. Ready for your grill. We'll see you for dinner."

"Shit, Lamb, as clear as they're coming in, they have to be within a rock's throw. They're at the most fifteen miles offshore. They're in the backyard. Let's get on over to Bubba's."

"Red Fox to Hawk, I'll put it on a standby. Be expecting you for dinner as soon as the sun's down. Red Fox out."

"Damn! We're on, Mike, tell me that Glen doesn't have some balls. We could probably see the boat from Horseshoe Beach. You wanna drive down there?"

"No, we've gotta get back to Bubba's. Well, shit, let's drive down to where we should be able to see the boat and take a real quick peep."

We drove a few miles down the road to Horseshoe Beach, but all we could see was sawgrass. We were still stoked knowing the boat was within fifteen miles of our truck.

We went back to Bubba's, loaded his boat with our supplies and pulled the big fish scow around to tie onto it, ready to head out right after sunset.

THERE WERE SIX of us in the two-boat parade, three in Bubba's little inboard and three of us laid back in the oversized fish scow, that looked more like a barge. It was so big, you could run laps in it.

We made contact right after dark, with no problem locating the boat, tying up, and beginning the unload. With the six of us and the three men on board, we were nine men working hard, but it was still fifteen tons to unload. Although we worked for hours and were pulling thirty- to eighty-pound bales of pure buds out of her belly, it didn't seem to make a dent. When the big fish scow was stacked as high as possible without an avalanche, I looked into the hull.

We still had a solid six to eight feet of bales still in there. We'd only taken a third of her load.

Shit! Was this girl going to have a long labor or what? It was definitely going to be an all-nighter.

We ran up Rocky Creek and tied up the fish scow carrying a mountain of bales at a pine island just across from Horseshoe Beach. We were less than two hundred feet across the creek from where we would meet the 18-wheelers the next night.

Seven of us unloaded backbreaking bales for hours, stomping through calf-deep mud. Several times it pulled my boots right off my feet. We didn't have far to go but the going was tough.

We piled bales until they towered over us and the barge was empty. We covered the mound with tarps and hung a spring scale off a branch of a pine, to weigh the bales at a later time. Now to fill the fish scow to the max again and do it all over.

We had some work cut out for us. We contacted the boat and started digging into her for the second time. We had the fish scow and Bubba's boat so loaded we couldn't put another bale on board either one. And the boat still had the legs of that baby in her belly. There was a quarter to a third of the load still in the hole of the shrimper.

Shit. It's going to take three trips to unload her completely!

It was midnight and the tide had turned out. It would be getting lower all night and Rocky Creek got bone dry at dead low water. *Shit! Shit! Shit!*

We explained to Glen there was no way to do the whole load tonight. "We'll take this load in and unload it and do the third one tomorrow night. We'll meet you out here tomorrow at the same spot just after dark and get the rest. Take her offshore about twenty miles, get some sleep, and I'll give you a shout right after dark, so have your radio on.

"Mammal, stay on board with Glen. It's your birthday and there's no need you getting all muddy and breaking your back on your birthday. Don't say I never gave you nothing."

Big hugs and happy birthdays to Mammal, slapped Glen five, and we headed back to shore.

I didn't look forward to tromping another heap of herb again. I'd already lost a boot to the hungry mud and almost didn't find it. My foot was cut and bleeding from the oyster beds. And muling some of the heavier bales were getting the best of my strength. My back and shoulders didn't have much left. All of us were running short on power, but it was something that had to be done and the adrenaline would definitely get us through.

The moon was rising and the tide was dropping fast. About four hundred yards off the island the scow started to bump. We played basketball bouncing off the bottom for about fifty yards and then the mountain slammed dead aground, sucking into the mud like glue. *Fuck!*

We're dead aground in the water with hundreds of bales stacked ten to twelve feet high above anything else for miles and miles out here in the saw grass flats. Rocky Creek just produced a mountain out of saw grass that grew about three feet high. You could see this hump of a turtle for miles and we had less than two hours until daylight. *Damn!*

We unloaded Bubba's little boat and headed back to the fish house, tied up, jumped into the trucks and headed to Bubba's house where his wife met us with hot coffee, fat back and eggs.

Bubba was great people and he and his wife were country as a red hen and a dozen eggs.

We all were beat. We tried to get some sleep but fat chance of that with all the things running through our minds.

Everyone laid up for a few hours resting our backs from last night's work. It took a toll on all of us. Bubba gave Rusty, Barry, Mike, Strings and me a ride down to Horseshoe Beach where we had one of the black Zodiac rafts hidden in the saw grass. We eased over to the pine swamp island, pulled the raft up onto dry land and began to weigh and count the bales on the big spring scale we had hanging from a tree.

We'd lift a bale and hang it. Get a reading and then spray paint the weight on to the bale. Mike used an adding machine with a roll of paper attached to it. We gave him a weight, he'd punch in the weight and it appeared on the paper—*36, 42, 21, 38, 80, 35, 19* and so on. We stayed there until after midday weighing and loading the herb to get it ready for the trucks to come in after dark. When finished, Mike had a long stretch of paper with 318 bales on it. The total weight was a hair over nine thousand pounds.

"Break open those cookies, Lamb," Barry shouted. "I'm starving."

"You're not the only one," Rusty said. "How about some sardines with those cookies."

"I'm not the chef, guys. Get what you want out of the bag. We've got plenty of cookies, and there are two dozen cans of sardines. Get what you want. There's plenty of water, too."

We sat down and attacked the bag, eating Happy Jack cookies, sardines and drinking water. The tide was still out but had turned in. Bubba stopped across the creek and gave us a beep from the truck.

"Weevil, you and Korn Dog get over there in those tall pines and keep an eye on the scow," Mike said. "I'm taking Rusty and Strings with Bubba to see what's going on with the trucks."

"If Big Jim and Kelly have any Gainesville boys with 'em, send them down, too. We're gonna need all the help we can get. We've got to load their trucks and we've still got seven or eight thousand we need to bring in."

"I know. Don't worry, Lamb. I'll get things straightened out. You and Barry keep an eye on the reefer."

Barry and I climbed a tree with about five pounds of weed in a wax paper bag and a couple of packs of matches. We didn't have the pot to smoke. We had it to burn, to keep away the clouds of mosquitoes while we kept an eye on the mountain of marijuana.

SIXTEEN

BARRY AND I sat in three or four different trees, easing closer to our mound of marijuana in the scow. Around three in the afternoon we finally reached the last tree and were at the water's edge. Our twelve-foot tall mound of pot sat about 150 yards in front of us, right in the middle of solid three-foot high saw grass.

Our mound rose about ten feet above the grass.

If we could just hang in there for another three hours, the tide would be in and night would fall.

Suddenly, out of nowhere, a military fighter jet screamed across the grass flats fifteen to twenty feet off the water, almost knocking the top bale out of the fish scow.

It was so loud and fast I thought I got shot. Shit.

"Fuck! We're busted!" I yelled. "The Air Force just flew over that pile of marijuana. You know they had to have seen that!" He was so close I could see the pimples on the kid's face. My heart was twenty yards away, hiding in the palmetto bushes.

But as it was, it must have been a youngster taking a low-flight joyride. *Thank you, God.*

Another hour passed. An overcast and fog started sliding in across the marshes. Barry and I looked at each other and smiled, lighting our five-pound bag of mari-juana to keep the skeeters off our asses.

"I guarantee there are some stoned bugs flying around these swamps," he said.

The sun was getting low into the horizon.

"Just a few more hours and we'll have it made, Korn Dog. Not too long, now." I was happily in my thoughts of big money, when I heard it.

"What's that?" The sound of a kicker motor getting close. "What the hell?"

"Look. To the north."

All I could see was a sailboat mast coming out of the next cut, about a half a mile to the north. It was a hell of a rig. A gill-net boat with the engine up front, a net table in the stern, and a mast sticking right up the middle of the boat. I held my breath. It turned away from us and the pile of weed. They were headed the other way.

Yeah, sure. Until one of them local boys spotted a new mountain out in the middle of their fishing grounds.

They turned and headed straight for the mound. They pulled up next to it and one guy jumped off his boat onto the fish scow. He grabbed a bale and jumped back on to his boat.

"*SHIT!* Those gill-netters found the mound!"

Barry and I jumped down and ran our asses off up to the main gravel road. There was no traffic. We walked for over a half an hour and then a car—well, it *was* a ride. A woman in a big long hearse pulled over.

"You boys want a ride?"

I didn't care if there was a coffin in there or not. "Sure do," I replied. "We need to get to nineteen."

"Well hop in then," she said. "Goin' that way m'self."

Thank God. She let us out on Route 19 and we started thumbing again. After a while a guy in a pickup stopped. A few miles later I spied Mike in Bill Allen's truck, the blue Ford we drove up in from Indian Rocks.

"Thanks, we'll get out here," I said to the driver, keeping my eye on Mike who was crossing the median in the center of 19, jumping to the northbound side. There were two 18-wheelers at a little off-cut truck-stop kind of spot, so small the two trucks completely filled it.

Barry and I ran across four lanes of traffic to the trucks. I told Mike and Big Jim, who was driving a big Cadillac and was in charge of the two transports what had happened.

"Fuck!" Mike said. "We gotta let Bubba know!"

Barry and I jumped in to the back of the pickup. Jim Maslanka drove the Cadillac. We arrived at Capo's. I described the boat to Bubba.

"No problem," he said. "We're neighbors. "Let's pay 'em twenty-five thousand to help us unload and use their boat. That will put a new tin roof on their house, which they need very badly."

"You sure they'll help us?" Mike asked.

"For *sure,*" Bubba said. "They've never seen that much money in their lives."

So we all loaded into the blue pickup and the Cadillac and went with Bubba, except for one of the helpers who had had enough. He was done with the deal and stayed behind at Bubba's. I won't name him because he never got busted.

The rest of us headed back to Horseshoe Beach to make sure the skiff was alone and all right. Bubba would go to the house of his neighbors', the ones who had found the barge and taken a bale, and make the deal with them to use their boat and help us unload. What a relief I felt.

Last night had taken its toll on us. We were all exhausted. As soon as I hit the floor of the truck bed, I was out.

SEVENTEEN

"YOU IN THE BACK OF THE TRUCK!" a voice shouted. "PUT YOUR HANDS UP AND GET OUT."

Now that made me wake up quick! I was so tired the Florida trooper must have been yelling awhile before I came around to the realization that it was the law barking out the music and that music was definitely the blues.

Another four-door unmarked car showed up. It was Florida Department of Law Enforcement. The two cars of law enforcement were yelling at the truck.

I looked up at the sound of another car coming. Big Jim was wheeling around the corner. When he saw the cops, he stopped, turned the Cadillac around and slammed the pedal to the metal.

The unmarked car took off after him.

The Florida Highway Patrol drew down on us.

"You in back of the truck. Put your hands up and climb out slowly, one at a time. You in the cab. Don't move. Put your hands out the window where I can see them."

I had rabbit running through my blood but common sense won out. The cop was as frightened as we were. Five of us and only one of him, way out in the swamps.

He didn't try and cuff us; he didn't have five sets of cuffs. He sat us all down at the back of the truck and held his cannon on us until along came the Caddy with an escort of police cars close behind. The cops flowed in like pigeons to popcorn. We were definitely busted.

They handcuffed our hands behind our backs to the handles of their car doors.

"Answer a few questions," one of the troopers said, "and we'll get you away from these mosquitoes and let you sit in the back of our cars.

"Where you boys from?"

"Florida," someone answered.

"What are you doing in these neck of the woods?"

"Just come up to do a little fishing with a friend of ours," Mike replied.

"Yeah, what're you fishin' for?"

"Whatever bites."

"How 'bout these mosquitoes. You gettin' any bites from them?"

"Yeah, I don't even have to use bait," I mumbled.

"You boys are the bait. And until you wanna tell me what the hell you're doin' down here in these woods, you'll continue to feed these thirsty little vampires. Answer a few questions and I'll put you in the back seat of the cruiser, or at least cuff you in the front where you can get 'em off your face.

"You boys look awful muddy, wet and rundown. You sure you're up here just fishin'? . . . No one's in a talking mood? You like those mosquitoes, huh?"

"Let them mosquitoes suck those boys dry," his partner said. "They're gonna play dumb and keep their mouths shut. We've got just the place for y'all."

"Well, well, who we got here? Mister Capo. Big Bubba. You takin' all these boys fishin'? Where's your boats?"

"They're at the fish house. We're just checkin' the tide and lookin' for some bait."

"Well, that's not what we heard. Some neighbor friends of yours reported seeing your boat just off Horseshoe Beach, run aground bone dry, right in Rocky Creek. In fact, they said it was loaded slam-full of potato sacks full of *mar-i-juana*. They even brought us one in. And boys, you sure made our day.

"The FDLE was in town making a half-pound bust of another completely different case. So when your neighbors called in what they found on your boat, the heat was already in town. The guys that found it didn't really know what it was, but *we* do."

It was probably a dream come true for them in Dixie County to make a half-pound buy, and now stumble onto tons of herb.

"So Bubba, we got a new mound of it. What're got to say about that? Bubba, you ain't got nothin' to say? You like those mosquitoes? How 'bout you, Red? You ain't got nothin' to talk about?"

"Yeah, let's go fishing."

"Oh, listen here, a smart ass. Sonny, what you don't realize is we are fishin' and it looks to me like we've caught a bunch. You're gonna . . ."

I'm going to drown in these mosquitoes. They're up my nose. In my mouth. Plugging my ears. Damn! Look at Barry. He's turned black on me.

"Hey, Red! You listenin' to me? Have you heard a thing I've said to you?"

"No. No sir. I haven't." I wasn't listening to him. All I could think about was being bled to death.

"Hey, Sarge, you guys getting anything out of those other boys. Can't get a thing outta Red."

"Not a thing."

"Well, you know there had to be a big mother boat. Where do you reckon it is?"

"It's probably headed for Cuba right now. Who the hell knows?"

"You know them boys know. You know it's not their marijuana. They have to be working for some big Mafia organization. Or some kind of organized crime."

They would never believe the truth if we told it to them.

"Lamb, lean over," Barry whispered. "I've got to wipe my face off on your shoulder. These mosquitoes are driving me nuts."

"Here, that's as far as I can lean. Okay, lemme borrow your shoulder now."

"What's wrong, boys? Y'all getting' tired of giving blood? You boys got more black on you than you do white. You know that back seat would be awful sweet. There ain't no skeeters in there."

No one answered. They think they've got a bunch of marijuana on the scow; wait until they find the other herb already weighed up and ready to go. It will take half the law enforcement in Florida to drag it out of the mud-surrounded pine island.

Finally they took the seven of us to Dixie County Jail. It was a big house that the sheriff lived in with a jail attached to the side. His wife cooked the food in her own kitchen and passed it through a side kitchen window to the people in the jail. The seven of us had the whole place to ourselves. Not that it was that big. There were only four four-man cells.

After two days the feds came into the game and took all our clothes to the lab. We were all dressed out in jailhouse jumpsuits and finally had a bond set. A hundred and twenty-five thousand, each. Denny, my friend who started me with lids, ten for a hundred, was there for me. He put my bond money up. For the moment, I paid him back with a smile and a lot of thanks.

The beach went nuts after we got out. Reporters, girls, and friends we never knew we had were following us up and down Gulf Boulevard, beeping their horns and waving. It was as if we were celebrities. As things settled, and we were out on bond, no one seemed concerned. Offers to do more gigs flowed in.

Mammal had dropped out of sight and it was weeks before we heard from him, but it was sweet when we did. He'd taken the pot north and the money he brought back helped pay for the lawyers, and Mike and I took care of the others that went down. Everyone needed help.

Mammal told us that the boat had come back the next night for us to unload.

"It was a blessing the wind blew and the seas got rough that night," he said. "We waited for hours, but never heard from the Red Fox. Then we saw a light on the horizon, bouncing all over. It never shut off. We knew it wasn't you guys so we pulled back offshore and headed south."

He had filled the two twenty-one-foot rafts with seven thousand pounds of herb and came in Clearwater Pass and headed four miles south down the Intracoastal waterway to the triplex on Indian Rocks Beach. Bill, Mammal and another guy ran seven thousand pounds across a vacant sandlot and across an empty road into their apartments. Not a pound got wet or busted.

Our friend, John Carroll, concerned about our bust, hooked us up with Percy Foreman, the famous defense attorney from Texas, who made a name for himself representing defendants in high profile murder cases.

In the meantime, I needed to make money to help the friends who were busted with us. I felt I had no alternative other than continuing to smuggle. I had to do at least a few more trips while out on bond.

This time I had a good unload. No more unloading in the swamps. It was a shrimp house in Georgia that Glen was hooked up with. And this time, my balls were on the line. If I got caught, I'd do the rest of my life in prison. Since I couldn't leave the country, I had Mammal see Boobs and he loaded the boats.

But even if I couldn't leave the country, I sure could unload straight from a boat into trucks and vans on dry land. That was the way to do it.

I built my financial situation back to a comfortable level, took care of my mother and family, and was off to court.

EIGHTEEN

COURT WAS A circus in itself. There were seven of us and we all had individual lawyers, with Percy Foreman the lead attorney. With seven individual lawyers, they could cross-examine seven times more than the prosecution.

Foreman, with his famous background and used to being in the limelight argued often with the judge.

"Mr. Foreman, you're not in Texas," Judge Middebrook told him more than once. "This is Florida and my court. Open your mouth one more time and I'll hit you with contempt of court."

"Your Honor, I don't care what courtroom or state this is. The law reads that . . . " and so on.

It was a daily verbal battle.

The judge never believed it was seven young men that organized this multi-million-dollar operation. And with a world-renowned lawyer, and friends such as John Carroll and his wife, Lucille, sitting right behind us, along with a packed courtroom of friends and family, many standing, Judge Middlebrook seemed to be in awe. The media coverage, and outpouring of support of friends, was overwhelming.

His Honor did not appear to be enjoying this circus at all. Bubba would fall asleep and begin snoring so loud the judge would have to stop all proceedings and ask if we could wake him up. This happened at least a half a dozen times a day. Big Bubba was almost forty, a giant of a man, six and a half feet tall and weighing well over three hundred pounds. The rest of us were in our twenties.

In Gainesville, every day after court it was a full-on party. The weekend of our trial, we all paraded home in a line of cars, family, friends and media. Once at home it was sex, partying and rock 'n roll. It might be our last time for a while to have bodily exercise with a woman. So it was around-the-clock sex, partying and time with our families.

Saturday night we all got together and went to the Crown Lounge. And of course, there was a big barroom brawl. A guy broke a bottle and stuck Barry's right forearm when he put it up to block the bottle. We took him to the hospital and he received 135 stitches and his arm was wrapped in a cast. That went over very nice in Court on Monday. With Bubba's snoring and Barry's psychedelic-signed cast, I wondered what the jury was thinking. They seemed to look at us in amazement.

The prosecution was trying to make Bubba, dressed in old country clothes, kicking off his shoes every fifteen minutes and falling asleep almost every hour on the hour, into the kingpin of this million-dollar deal. Yeah. The truth of the matter was, this deal was the first time Bubba had ever seen pot.

And the six young men sitting beside him, uneducated mullet fishermen? (At twenty, I was the youngest.) Many people just knew the guilty ones weren't even in the courtroom. Had to be members of some big organization all dressed in black who were responsible and backing this venture. We were just young kids and an old country boy being used to take the fall for some big international organization.

The prosecution blew up a picture on a big movie screen showing how the paper found in Mike's pocket with the weights on it, matched it to the adding machine paper roll. Where it was ripped off, the two pieces fit like a fat tick on a yellow dog.

Another witness, a clerk at the little country store we stopped at, testified that she sold us sardines and Happy Jack cookies the day before we were arrested, which verified the things the police found right next to the mound of pot.

After a week and a half, on Wednesday, the eighth working day of the trial, it was time for closing arguments.

They never found a joint on us. It was all circumstantial evidence, but the pot and burlap debris found on all of our clothes, taken from us in Dixie County Jail, and the paper from the adding machine found in Mike's pocket, with 318 weights that matched the 318 bales piled up on the island, probably didn't help much. It was hard to read the jury as they filed out.

The judge then spoke to us. "I've figured this pot weight up and you boys had enough marijuana for every American to smoke a joint," Judge Middlebrook said. "You boys are known coast to coast for hauling the most." It wasn't hard to read his mind.

The trial took eight days, and it took the jury all day to come back with a verdict.

We were found guilty on all four charges.

NINETEEN

AT SENTENCING, WHILE one of us was being sentenced by the judge, another one would wait in the jurors' box to be the next one up. I was about the fourth in line. When I was sentenced, the judge stated that I was found guilty of all four counts containing the maximum of five years on each charge. He then told me he was sentencing me to five years running consecutively on each count.

"Do you have anything to say?"

"God bless you and have a good day," I replied.

When I returned to the holding cell in the back, my co-defendants asked me what I received. "Shit, he gave me five years." They were on my ass jumping all over me like kangaroos on a trampoline. "What?" "How?" "Did you snitch?" "What the hell?" "How'd you get that, Lamb?"

But then Maslanka, who was next in line after me, came to the holding cell. He'd gotten twenty years.

"How'd Lamb get five?" Mike asked.

Bubba joined in. "Yeah. What the hell's going on here?"

"Lamb didn't get five years," Maslanka said. "He got five years *consecutive*." He looked at me. "That means five years *four times over*, Lamb. You do five, then start a second five, then a third, then a fourth one. You got five years all right." He laughed. "Four fives running wild.

Equals twenty years, you dumb ass. You got the same as us."

"Twenty years? Damn it! I'm twenty years old. That's as long as I've been living. Got twenty years? They busted us with twenty thousand pounds. I'm twenty years old. What's with all these twenties?"

"Well, I guess it's three squares, a bunk and a punk," Mike said.

"Yeah. I doubt that. I ain't going that route. Maybe three hots and a cot and it's rent free. They'll pay for our water, electricity, medication, feed us and do our laundry. But there ain't none of this bunk and a punk shit with me."

The seven of us received 130 years total. Six of us each got twenty years. Rusty, from Pass-A-Grille, was sentenced to ten; guess the judge thought he wasn't as involved. He was right: Rusty was a good man, really not into the business like us others. He just wanted to get involved in a trip and taste the excitement. Well, he got a taste. He received the full buffet. All he could eat.

Rusty's father was the mayor of St. Pete Beach at the time. A little something more for the papers to write about.

Judge Middlebrook denied all motions for bond. We were sent to the Leon County Jail and put in maximum lockdown.

Meanwhile, I was visited by my friend, Lisha, who introduced me to two lawyer friends of hers, Joe O'Terry and Marty Weinberg of the Boston firm, O'Terry and Weinberg.

They promised they could get us an appeal bond and we would be out within a week. "Plus I'll give you this gold Rolex on my wrist when you get out," O'Terry said. "We'll come pick you up."

"Just get my friends and me out. That's all I want right now."

ALL SEVEN OF us were downstairs in a big, open area behind the Control Room. I was scared to death. What was
going to happen to me? Who was I going to get locked
up with? I stayed close to the others. We all tried to stay
together and pick out who we wanted to be in the cells
with. I wanted to be with Barry, Rusty or Strings, somebody mellow. Mike and Jim weren't happy at all. They
kept yelling at each other about whose fault it was and
why we got busted. I didn't want to be locked in a cell
with either one of them. But someway, somehow—I don't
know what happened or what I was doing—I turned
around and before I realized it, everyone was headed
upstairs. Except Bubba and me. My heart took a fart.

We were led to a cell near the control room on the
bottom floor. The guard opened a solid steel door, in the
center of which was a small diamond-shaped window.
Just below was a little food trap about the length and
width of a shoe box. He pushed me in a cell that was
dark and full of smoke. My first step I tripped over a leg
but there was no body attached to it. *What the hell is going on?* As thoughts were flying through my head, Bubba
was pushed in right behind me. I took three steps and
was immediately stopped by the rear wall, which was
solid steel. The entire cell was solid steel, three steps by
two steps. I felt like I was in a square can. Standing between the bunks, I reached out on either side of me and
touched each bunk at the same time. Two steel bunks
welded on each side of the walls with a steel sink that
ran into a steel toilet in between the bunks. Everything
was steel. Over the shitter was a light bulb with a steel
screen around it. As I looked, there was that leg again.
The leg, a black one, was leaning against the toilet and
the leg's owner was sitting on one of the bottom bunks.
He was heating up a wax milk carton with coffee in it.

The wax protected the carton from catching on fire, but it filled the little steel box with smoke and soot. In the first minutes I spent in jail I tripped over a leg with no body attached to it in a sooty, smoke-filled room with two black guys heating up coffee in an orange juice carton. This was going to be one helluva trip, I knew.

The two black guys had the bottom bunks. I jumped up on one of the top bunks. Bubba was too big and weighed way too much to get up and down from the other top bunk, so he traded the two-legged black guy his top bunk for the bottom one.

It was hell. Adding to all that was going on, Bubba had a big boil-type thing at the end of his spine that had to do something with his open heart surgery. I had to drain it every day for him because no one else would help him. Talk about nasty!

That light in the cage over the shitter stayed on all the time, so I didn't know if it was day or night. The only way I could tell time was by the meals. And I never knew what day it was. There was no music, nothing to read, no place to exercise. I lay on a hot, hard-assed bunk with no pillow or blanket all day, all night. I was young and used to going out every night, even on Monday nights. Partying with girls, drugs and rock 'n' roll. I had a king-sized bed, pillows, air conditioning. I was used to the good life.

I sure hoped O'Terry and Weinberg would come through on their promises.

The only way to tell days of the week was by the two days we had visitors and the two days we got to shower. The shower was next to the Control Room. That turned out to be a blessing.

When visitors came, they visited us in our cells, looking through the dirty little diamond-shaped window. They used the same bathroom that we showered in next to the Control Room. After the first few visits, girls I knew put reefer, papers and Quaaludes under the sink in the bathroom. I'd load up on every shower day.

Boy, did I look forward to those showers.

Smoking a little herb and eating a few Quaaludes really helped pulling time. After all, having to sit in that cell, dank and dirty and dark—we'd wrapped newspapers around that damn light—there wasn't anything else to do but lie on the bunk and think. I lay up in that little steel box so long feeling like I was holding my breath underwater.

Bubba and I had so many visitors that our cell mates didn't have time or a chance to see their visitors, so they complained to the guards and the guards moved them and brought down Mike and Jim. This made things worse.

Those two were at each other's throats, and both of those guys were too tough to fight each other because someone would definitely be killed. So they took out all their frustration and stress on me.

"Lamb, been waitin' to get down here with you," Mike said, "and stomp your ass all over this cell. Yeah, I heard you and Nancy had some things goin' on just before we went to court."

"Mike, what're you talking about? I never had an affair with Nancy. You know she loves you. She's like a sister to me. Where the hell did you hear this shit?"

"He heard it from Cathie and some of the beach chicks that came up to visit us," Maslanka said. "He's fuckin' nuts, Lamb. He's losing it."

"Fuck you, Maslanka. It's your fuckin' fault we're even—"

"B-b—*boys!*" Bubba shouted. "Just stop this here nonsense right now. I'm gettin' plumb tired of listenin' to all this hogwash. Whose fault it is and whose fault it ain't. We all here in prison togeth—."

189

"My fault? Knight, I wouldn't even be here if it wasn't for you. Just lay off Lamb."

"Fuck you, Jim! I'll—"

The fists were flying and the bodies were being slammed on steel bunk corners and concrete floors.

"Hot damn, boys, I told you all to cut this stupid shit," Bubba yelled, rolling out of his bunk, pushing Mike one way and Maslanka the other.

These were some rough times and with twenty years on my back, everyone was saying it would only get worse. Shit. I didn't know how it could get any worse than this.

But Mike and Jim were persuading me with their stories that it soon would.

"Yeah, Lammie Pie, they're goin' to love your sweet pink ass in prison. All them queers just waitin' on the stairway to butt-fuck a cute little blond-haired boy like you."

"Mike's right. Wait 'til you take your physical, Lamb. They're gonna give you an enema."

"An enema? What the hell's an enema?"

"Oh, yeah, honey," Mike said and laughed. "You're gonna find out what an enema's all about."

"Quit bullshittin'. Really, what's an enema?"

"Weevil, they gotta clean your system out before they let you go into general population. They'll stick a hose bellybutton deep up your ass and turn on hot, soapy water, which will make you shit all over yourself. Then you'll be laying there butt-naked with shit all over you and everybody looking and laughin' at you."

"Screw you guys. You're gonna get the same if they do it to me, you're gonna get the exact same thing."

"Oh, no, they won't do it to us. They're only going to give it to you, because you're only twenty."

"Fuck off, Paper Ass. And Mike, you look as young as I do."

"That's enough, boys!" Bubba yelled. "Just stop that dumb shit. Leave Steve alone. You boys ain't gonna have no picnic either. In fact, we all in a heap'a shit. And it ain't nothin' to be funnin' around with. Now just stop this foolishness. I don't feel like hearin' it."

A LITTLE OVER a month of that county shit in the little steel box, I was scared to death, but almost happy, to be the first one of us seven ordered out.

"Cuff up, Lamb. You're going to the penitentiary."

I knew I was in for an experience of a lifetime.

I was a federal prisoner. This meant that the feds could send me anywhere in the country, out of state, far from my family and friends. They could ship me up north to New York; out to California; Atlanta; to Lewisburg; Leavenworth; El Reno; even to Seattle. There was no telling where I was going to go.

Came the big day and I went right across town, to the Tallahassee FCI, Federal Correctional Institution.

TWENTY

HELL, IT WAS like being released. The prison was made up of dorms and had a big rec yard, a third of a mile running track, two handball courts, a football field, two baseball fields, a soccer field, eight basketball courts, and a huge weight pile. Did I want a Hitachi boom box? I could buy one in the commissary. Did I want ice cream? There were all kinds, plus anything else I wanted to eat. I could lie out at Butt Beach and get a tan, if I wanted. I could watch movies on the weekend, eat food every bit as good as in a restaurant. The place was unreal, like a college with no women. Well, I take that back. They did have women. The Medical Department had a few fine nurses. There were some good-looking schoolteachers right out of the college in Tallahassee. A few of my friends had love affairs with some of them.

I was in heaven compared to the county jail, and it only got better when the word got out that I was one of the Steinhatchee Seven. I had friends I didn't even know; people offered me all types of things.

Plus I had a twenty-year sentence. A large percent of the sentences there were only six years—Zip 6s. Bank robbers, who made up about 25 percent of the population, had sentences of up to fifteen years. One other guy had a twenty-year sentence, the same as mine, for a shooting. And the only guy who had more time than me was John. He had a thirty-year sentence for heroin smuggling.

I lived for our appeal, praying to the Good Lord that he would bless us somehow and some way, and that we wouldn't have to spend twenty years of our lives in prison.

Yeah, Tallahassee was much better than the county jail. But I was all alone; none of my co-defendants were here. I wondered about my friends, my homeboys. Where were they? Where were they being sent? What part of the country? Once I could make phone calls to my family, and people knew where I was, mail and visitors started showing up. Burr Louis, a Cortezan fisherman and a very good friend, made sure I got a copy of the *St. Petersburg Times* every day. One day a prison buddy told me, "One of your rap partners is in R and D, Receiving and Discharging. His name is Rusty."

"No shit?" I flew down there. It was true. My lifelong friend—the one with the ten-year sentence—was here.

Once he was situated, we walked the yard, talking about the truckload of time we were pulling.

"They've got a good case against us," he said. "I expect we'll have to do the whole stretch."

I didn't want to hear it. I still had faith that something would happen and I'd be out of here sooner than later.

Rusty and I adjusted to the months going by as we lived the same routine every day. We spent more time in the visiting room than we did in the prison. I had a visit from a female friend of mine. As we were talking, she told me, "I have a gift for you. Balloons filled with buds, all cleaned and ready to roll."

"What?" I said. "A balloon? I have to be strip searched after every visit. I'm not taking that thing in with me."

"There's a little pack of Vaseline with it," she whispered. "You just keester it. Put it up your ass."

"Up my ass? Are you nuts?"

"*Shhh!* You won't feel it. They'll be the first things out. Just clean 'em off and break the balloon and you'll have plenty of smoke. And I put in some Quaaludes, seven-fourteens, for you, too."

I'll be damned if I wasn't in that bathroom sticking three fucking balloons knuckle deep up my ass.

Now it's strip search time. What'll happen? Did I use too much Vaseline? Will he see the grease around my ass? God! Did I wipe it all off?

"Next!"

Great Lord. I was scared, standing there butt-naked with a belly full of balloons and a greased up backside. All I wanted to do was get to a toilet.

"Lamb, behind your ears. Run your fingers through your hair. Open your mouth. Lift your tongue. Lift your nut sack. Turn around. Bottoms of your feet. Bend over. Spread those cheeks."

Omigod!

"Give me a big cough."

I spread my cheeks. Damn! What if a balloon comes shooting out my suitcase and hits him right between the eyes. I coughed. *Nothing happened.* Oh, thank you, Lord. *Thank you,* Lord!

"Lamb, get dressed. Next."

After the strip search, I went straight to the shitters. There were no stalls, just toilets side by side. It was still work call; no one else was in the bathroom.

They shot out like canaries through an open window. I cleaned them all off in the sink with hot soapy water. I broke the balloons and Rusty and I partied that night.

After that, most every visit was a balloon visit. I had six or eight inmate buddies without any friends or family to visit, so I had them put my female friends on their visitor lists. At times it seemed like half the prisoners in the visiting room, were collecting balloons for me.

I had at least a pound stash of pot and a bag of pills at all times.

With a stash that big, I needed Posey, the strongest white boy in the prison, holding my drugs. Posey was a weightlifter and as straight as an arrow. I met him when he stole my brand new prison-issued clothes.

He worked in the warden's office. He stashed all my drugs behind the drawers in the warden's desk. Posey brought down whatever I ordered for the night's party. Half the population was stoned out after the evening chow. It was easy time.

I did have a few problems with a few greedy and jealous inmates, but things were handled.

I had no problem sleeping at night, a few Valiums and a nice joint or two, was almost more than an inmate could ask for. But I had another need, just as important. That worked out, too.

The inmates' bathroom was right next to the visitors'. Thank God for drop ceilings. And the guys before me who passed on the information. One of my girl friends went into the visitors' bathroom, I went into the inmates' bathroom, jumped onto the toilet, then onto the sink. I lifted a square of the ceiling out and climbed over the wall. And yes, a real woman. The best remedy to get rid of a pair of blue balls. I climbed back over the bathroom divider and walked out with a giant smile upon my face. This made time much easier. Sex, drugs and rock 'n roll in the federal pen.

There was always a line of prisoners waiting to go into the bathroom. Eventually the guards got hip, and after about a year, they welded the roof shut. It was great while it lasted.

Life was routine: A job in Auto Mechanics VT Trade. Working out on the weight pile. Running miles of dirt under my feet. Playing handball and getting in tiptop shape. Then just before count time, we burned a few joints, ate a Quaalude or a few Valiums and off we went to sleep for another day.

One day a guy came up to me.

"I wanted to shake your hand," he said. "In fact, I'm here on behalf of your load. I was an MP, military

police. My friends and I were guarding the Army bunkers your pot was in. We took out the air conditioner and slipped out fifteen hundred pounds of it. I got busted selling it to a fed on the streets. I just wanted to meet you. I know there was a good twenty thousand pounds when they busted it. It's amazing how it just dwindled away to a smaller amount."

That was satisfying to hear. At least it wasn't all trashed.

I stayed deep in prayer and kept the faith. Thank God for my family, who never gave up on me. Mom and my sisters visited me as often as they could, once or twice a month. Sometimes even Nana made the trip.

It was a hardship, I know, but Mom always said, "Steve, you're only twenty. Don't worry. Just pray to the Good Lord. Like I always tell you, I know He has a purpose for you and things will work out. I'm just so sad and heartbroken that you're in here."

"Mom, don't cry. Look, I tattooed a little smile on my calf." I pulled up my pant leg. "I'm always smiling. I'll die with a smile, Mom."

Although I tried hard to convince her I was in good spirits, it wasn't always easy to pretend. Particularly when I knew the visits tore her up.

And then one day, on about our fourteenth month, our appeal came back. We won on two counts of our charges! O'Terry and Weinberg had worked a miracle!

We were re-sentenced and received a ten-year YCA Youth Act. We would see the next parole board. When that day came I had about fifteen months in. My guidelines were sixteen months' prison time with eight years' paper. I was given a release date in forty-five days.

It didn't work that way for the others.

Rusty received a year put off, a review in one year. Jim Maslanka was in Lewisburg. He was put off the maximum for three years. Mike Knight was in Terre Haute. He received a put-off, a review in three-years. Strings received eighteen months. Barry Korn was in El Reno, Oklahoma. He wouldn't see the parole board for another eighteen months. Bubba was in Atlanta Federal Penitentiary. He received a three-year put-off.

We all had the same record and never been in trouble before. There was no reason I should be given a forty-five-day date while some of my partners, guilty of the same rap, were put off for three years before they could even see the parole board again. This wasn't right. I appealed my forty-five days and lost my date.

The lawyers complained that they had to spend time and money flying from one side of the country to the other because their clients were incarcerated in different prisons in different states. The Court agreed and put six of us in Tallahassee. Bubba stayed in Atlanta.

It was almost like being back on the beach. With all of us in one place, having visitors almost every day, partying whenever we wanted, and the Commissary crew being all Steinhatchee, it was as if we ran the place. It was nuts.

Three months later we saw the parole board on their next meeting and we were all given the same release date. The night before our day to leave, we had one helluva of a party.

"Lamb, Lamb, they're calling your name," someone shouted at me the next morning. "Get your ass up out of bed. Don't you want to go home?" I was still loaded from the reds I ate the night before, but came to real quick.

Mom and my sisters, along with Nancy, Mike's girlfriend, flew up with the lawyer in his private plane, and were at the prison door when we got out. We all flew back, one big happy family, to St. Petersburg's Albert Whitted Airport to start living a free life once again.

I'd done twenty months—those twenties again. But thank God those twenties were behind me.

Sometimes—
the big ones
just didn't make it

So—
there was
plenty of meat
for the people

and good size jaws for
the walls

TWENTY-ONE

AS SOON AS I returned home, the first place I headed was to the water. I'd dreamed of swimming almost every day and finally it was time for a one-and-a-half off the dock.

I moved into the back bedroom of my mother's house. It was a nice setup. I could shut the door and keep my room private, and had an entrance from the outside, as well.

I got a job at the Aquatarium. I loved the job and I learned a lot. We caught dolphin and pre-trained them as show dolphin and to interact with humans. Some went to Orlando Sea World and others stayed in our aquarium.

I also caught fish for the viewing tanks, fishing under a permit, always having a marine patrol officer on board when catching dolphin. It was usually Harry Spivey, a marine patrol officer from St. Pete and a great guy, well liked by most all the fishermen.

The main tank at the Aquatarium contained a pilot whale with some high-jumping dolphin. Later the Aquatarium became Shark World, and that main tank became a shark tank, filled with a reef of giant boulders. My job was to catch sharks and to keep them alive. It was much harder to keep a shark alive than a dolphin. Unlike sharks, dolphin have a blow hole and breathe air. Sharks, on the other hand, cannot survive long out of water. Once a shark was caught, we had to slide at least its head and gills into a box I'd built on the back of my boat, that held less than two feet of oxygenated water. Many times we had to use a stretcher due to their size and weight. The biggest one I caught was a twelve-foot female tiger shark, but I returned her to the Gulf when she wasn't doing well in captivity.

Along with Shark World came a zoological garden that housed a dozen large cats: tigers, lions, jaguars, and three black leopards raised from cubs. A friend, Jim, and I took care of the cats. We cleaned the cages daily, getting in the cages with the lions and leopards. We even took the black leopards to the beach out back to swim and exercise. The other cats we had to put in catch pens when entering the cage. I learned a lot catching dolphin, working with large cats, sharks, and a fifteen-foot crocodile. I also cleaned the alligator pits, which held up to fifty alligators in each one. The job at the Aquatarium gave me some income and life was grand. Parole wasn't so bad, after all, and I was doing the right thing.

But almost everyone I talked to seemed to be in the business, involved in one way or another in marijuana smuggling. People you would never think of, were coming to me and asking for help.

I learned in prison—where I had a lot of time to think—that a successful unload was what we hadn't had and was the reason we ended up busted.

Large gigs required a good unload. You could not tromp through the mud with bales on your shoulder and hide tons of marijuana in the swamps, just to come back in smaller boats and do the same thing all over again the next night, to tromp them back out through the mud and load them on trucks waiting along the sides of the road at the Skyway Bridge with cars passing by. This was nuts. To do a successful load you needed a fish house or a good deep water spot where you could pull the big boat and the transports right up to each other.

With all the press coverage and media we had, all sorts of people came to us.

"You and Mike can make things work, Stevie," one pillar of the community said. "I want to get in on making some serious money."

"You? You're thinking about gettin' into smuggling? I can't believe it. Hell, you don't need any money."

"Stevie. I will never have enough money."

"Believe me, I would love to help you. I really need some money myself. That bust definitely had me digging up the yard. I'm just about back to scratch. Besides, I'm pulling eight years federal parole. I've gotta walk a straight line and I love working at the Aquatarium."

My good character and dignity didn't last too long, however.

"Bo Weevil. Wanna get involved in a gig?" Mike asked one day. "Unload thirty thousand for me?"

"What've you got goin'? There's no way I'm even thinking about it if we don't have a good unload where we can pull the boat next to the trucks."

"I've got it covered. The unload is perfect. In fact, a good friend of ours, and you used to work for him on one of Hubbard's boats."

"Who we talking about and how secure is the unload?"

Mike looked at me and grinned. "Ralphie."

"Little Ralphie? Captain on the *Flying Fisherman*? No shit! He's got it goin' on?"

"You can fly up to Panama City tomorrow and check out the unload yourself. I'll have Ralph pick you up. Can you still get that plane we used to rent outta Albert Whitted?"

"Dunno. Haven't used it in a couple of years, but I know the guy well and he's still flying out of there, I believe."

"Check it out and let me know, 'cause I've got to send you up with a hundred grand. If you can't rent that plane we'll have to drive up."

"What's the hundred grand for?"

"It's for Ralphie."

"What about the Lambo? What kinda money you talkin' about paying me?"

"I'll give you two hundred and fifty grand and all the pot you can sell."

So much for all my good intentions.

THAT GIG REQUIRED my meeting a dozen Winnebagos in Panama City and orchestrating their loading in a little deep water cut just off the Intracoastal at a place called Mexico Beach—right across the street from a fire tower occupied twenty-four hours a day by a ranger.

After that, many other gigs followed. I don't know for sure what that ranger thought. Or the bridge tender, who opened his bridge for large shrimp boats headed to nowhere a shrimp boat should be going, only to return a few hours later.

I was out of prison and on federal parole and doing more tonnage of weed, and loading more pickups, campers, Winnebagos, 10-wheelers, 18-wheelers, and anything that would fit down that little dirt road, than I'd ever done in my entire life or ever believed possible.

Sometimes I stopped in the office of my parole officer in St. Pete, filled out my report, talked to him for awhile, then drove less than half a mile to Albert Whitted Airport and got on a private twin-engine plane and flew to Panama City, where Ralphie picked me up, received his grocery bag of unload money and took me to his house, so I would be ready to meet my shrimp boat, pregnant with bales, that was coming up the Gulf.

Things were becoming history at the unload site across the street from the ranger's station. In fact, much of the Panhandle was getting burned out. There might be fifty gigs a month, sometimes as many as three in a single night. It was just flat being abused.

It seemed everyone was unloading in the pine tree farms owned by the St. Joe Paper Company in Port St. Joe. Some of the guards at the fenced-in areas to the pulp wood pine forest had been paid off, and some fishermen had access to the deep-water where boats and trucks could meet side by side and be hidden in tall pines. Sometimes guards gave out keys; sometimes off-load crews cut the locks and let themselves in and out.

I knew it was time to get out of the Panhandle, but Ralphie persuaded me otherwise.

"Steve, don't stop yet. I've got a nice boat and a crew of local boys that'll go to Colombia. Can you get any more of that gold bud?"

"Too many people up here. I don't want to do any more unloads in the Panhandle. I'm gonna talk to a buddy of mine who has a fish house in Georgia."

"These are local boys. And it's a local boat. Comes and goes outta here all the time."

I shook my head. "Don't know, Ralphie. So many boats up here now. Sure you don't want to do something on the East coast?"

"No, Steve. These boys live here. And the boat is well known. Has a good name and shrimps hard. Has no heat on it. Shit, I'm gettin' on up in age. These are my neck of the woods. I'd just feel better shittin' in my own back-yard."

He unwrapped a cigar, snipped the end with his pock-etknife, put fire to it and looked me in the eye. "Let's do one more, Steve. I'll take care of you. I'll do you right."

If I was going to do one more, it was definitely going to be Colombian. "Okay, Ralphie. One more. As long as it's Colombian. Those damn Jamaican bales fall apart. It looks like a marijuana plantation at the end of Sparky's road."

"HELL, BOYS," RALPHIE'S wife, said, "it's two nights before the boat's in. Let's go to the wrestlin' match in town. They've got some real biggun's fightin' tonight."

"Steve, we're goin' to the wrestlin' match," Ralphie de-clared. "We don't miss a one if we can help it. Ma loves them wrestlers."

"Sounds good to me."

"Emma, you got your pistol?"

"You ever catch me without it? Got it right here in my purse."

We arrived at the Panama City Arena and had front row seats. These people lived for wrestling. During one heated match I thought Emma was going to have a heart attack. She was never in her seat, jumping up and down and yelling, starting arguments with rival fans who liked someone other than her favorite. This crowd of hilligans were definitely country folk.

"Crowbar him!" a young, blond-haired woman sitting behind us shouted. "Crowbar him!"

Those were the wrong words to say about Emma's hero. "Arena Rat," she shouted, "don't you say nothin' about him, Floozie." Pissed off, she turned back around and sat down. "Who does she think she is?" she asked, having already made up her mind as to who she was.

The last straw for Emma was when the blond woman's muscle-bound boyfriend ran his mouth about that wrestler of hers. That was it.

She stood up and turned around again. "You damn Yankee," she yelled, and swung her purse over her head and squarely onto the man's skull. It might have looked like a purse to an onlooker, but inside was that pistol she carried. She split the man's melon wide open.

The rest of the night Ralphie and I spent at the jail, bonding out Emma.

The next night was, thankfully, much more mellow. We had a cookout, and Emma was a great cook. She didn't fail to mention more than once, however, how that big bruiser needed to be put in his place. Ralphie reminded her, again more than once, "You're out on bond. You gotta quit totin' that pistol everywhere you go, sleeping with it and all. They catch you with that you go right back in jail. You got to be toeing the mark."

"Ain't like I'm robbin' banks, Ralphie. Just totin' it is all. I'll be damned if I'm givin' it up."

Ralphie smiled and shook his head. "That's my Emma, boy. Maybe someday you'll have one just like her. Iffen you're lucky."

THE NIGHT OF the unload was at hand. Ralphie and I were just walking out the door when the phone rang. He answered, listened, shook his head and shouted into the phone.

"Get someone back on that boat!" . . . "Whatta you mean you can't get back on it?" . . . "Get your fat asses back on that boat. Or somebody on it!" He hung up and turned to me.

"That's my cap'n. Him and the crew are at a bar downtown."

"What the fuck do you mean, *the crew's at a bar?* Who the hell's on the boat? Whatta you got? A bunch of drunks?"

"No, they're all good boys, Steve, but coming in the inlet, they had to back 'er down waiting for the bridge to open. Sheared a pin and the wheel fell off."

"Well what the fuck are they doin' in the bar? Whose on the boat?"

"Nobody."

"Nobody? What? We got a boatload of pot just floating under the bridge. Whatta you mean, *nobody?*"

"There was a hard in-coming tide and all they had was a spinnin' shaft and a screamin' motor. Ben threw the anchor over and the boat's on the hook right in the middle of the pass, fifty yards off the bridge."

"So why're they in the bar?"

"It's such a thin little pass," he said, "and right in front of the bridge. Chicken asses got scared and jumped. Threw over dive tanks, radio, anything with their names on it."

"Oh, they threw half the supplies over and left a seventy-two-foot hull full of pot floating right in front of God and the whole world? Let's go get 'em and go back to the boat."

We picked up two of the four guys, leaving the two who wanted nothing more to do with the deal. When we got to the pass the shrimp boat was anchored just off the bridge.

"No lights! No one on board! What the fuck were you guys thinking?" I yelled at the crew, ready to kick some ass. "What if a shrimper comes by? Or any boat for that matter. No lights on, nobody on board. Just a ghost boat floatin' in the middle of the pass. They can't even get by you. With somebody on board we could at least keep 'em off the boat, until Ralphie's friend gets here to tow us to safety."

I couldn't believe it wasn't busted yet. There was no bridge tender and no shrimp boats had passed by yet on their way to the big shrimp house and docks just inside the pass, 300 yards from where the boat was on the hook.

Somebody had to get on board and turn on some lights. Ralphie was too old. The two others were big-bellied hilligans. Shit, it was my skinny little ass that was going to have to climb the anchor rope upside down to get on board.

The freeboard on the side of the boat was a good eight feet high, and the crew left nothing hanging over to get back on to the boat with. They'd just jumped off the boat and hauled ass.

I climbed up the rope, turned on some lights and settled back to wait for Ralphie's friend and his boat. *What the hell have I got myself in to. I'm not even supposed to be on here. This is* Ralphie's *boat and his crew, and I'm the only one who can get back on it? I'm on federal parole, not supposed to leave Pinellas County, and here I am sitting on another load of pot stuck in the middle of a pass and watching cars drive over the bridge that won't open. Man, am I ate up with the dumb ass.*

Finally a big 65-foot sport fisherman pulled up next to me—and wouldn't you know it, the name was the *Flying Fisherman*—the same name as one of Hubbard's boats I worked on with Ralphie out of Pass-A-Grille when I was fourteen. It towed me for three hours up the Intracoastal to Sparky's unload where I met Ralphie and the crew and we finally unloaded the nightmare. I was definitely blanketed with God's Mercy.

But it was time to make a change. The Gulf and the Panhandle were becoming history. On the other hand, the East Coast was all ocean, thousands and thousands of miles of water. When you're in the Gulf, if you had a problem, you were in the Gulf. The Gulf is like a horseshoe, at the most, less than a thousand miles across; you're never *that* far from shore where you could be easily discovered. The Atlantic is much, much larger and offered a lot more open water in which to run your course.

I decided to visit Glen, my captain on the Steinhatchee boat who lived and shrimped all his life in Georgia.

TWENTY-TWO

"NO THANKS, STEVE. I'm not interested, but I can hook you up with some local boys who have their own boats and fish houses."

I could tell by looking at the mansion he was living in that smuggling wasn't what he wanted right now. I wouldn't want to lose such a fine place either.

I now had access to some of the best unloads available on the southeastern coast of the United States. These were deep water cuts that ran up to shrimp houses where tons of shrimp were unloaded on a daily basis into 18-wheelers that could back up to conveyor belts and collect shrimp from the hold of a boat. And right up those little dirt roads was direct access to the Interstate.

(If we'd had this on our Steinhatchee gig, we'd never been busted.)

PEOPLE WERE MAKING millions now and had the money to buy much larger loads, bigger boats and even small freighters. Some of the weights being ordered were forty to fifty tons at a shot. It was hard for the little rock of Jamaica to produce constant loads of that magnitude. Colombia, however, could give you whatever tonnage you needed. Plus, because of the superb packaging of Colombian herb, there was very little debris, if any, left in the bilge.

Besides that, Colombian blocks and bales were uniform in size and boats could hold a third more weight, while Jamaican packaging was never uniform. Jamaican marijuana was lightly compressed in second, third, fourth or even fifth generation—by then, rotten—potato sacks that often busted open as they were being passed out of the hold. At times crews had to shovel up to two thousand pounds of spilled seed and weed into fish boxes and dump them overboard.

Santa Marta was a Colombian mountain range, called the Sierra Nevada de Santa Marta and was full of marijuana plantations. If there was plenty of rain, the green fields produced a good commercial pot. But during a season of little rainfall or drought, the plants dried on the root and turned a bright yellow.

Santa Marta Gold Bud or Colombian Gold produced a hashy taste and was one of the best tasting pots I've ever smoked and was sought out by all buyers.

The years of 1975 and '76 were dry years in the Santa Marta region. And very good years for business.

TWENTY-THREE

AS THE POPULAR Columbian Gold Bud flowed into the country, a lot more money flowed into my hands. I bought a three-bedroom house on Sunset Beach for cash. Sun Dog, my Golden Retriever, who I'd bought as a puppy, loved that house on the water.

He could dive up to thirty feet underwater, holding his breath almost a minute. He also barked mathematical answers, never missing a number.

"Give me a number," I'd ask someone.

"Three into twenty-one."

Sunny barked seven times.

Amazed onlookers thought I was giving him hand signals, and made me hold my hands behind my back. Still Sunny barked the right answers.

He became a legend, the most talked-about dog on the beach. I would cruise down the pass and people would say, "There goes Lamb with his eagle and his counting dog."

In the back yard was the eagle, Adidas, a Bonelli's South African Eagle that I received from Bob

Campbell, the head veterinarian at the Aquatarium, after I got a federal permit to keep him. I trained him for falconry, a hobby I loved.

He was in a huge cedar cage I could walk in, that I had built by Marty Murray. Tied up at the dock, off my seawall on Blind Pass, were three boats—one, named *Happy Days*, I had built by ChooChoo, a Cuban boat builder on Stock Island next to Key West, a thirty-seven-foot Number One Hull with a brand new 3208 turbo caterpillar; the first twenty-two foot big block inboard Lafitte Skiff built by Jeff Stitt of St. Pete; and a little net boat, a Tremblay I used to catch mullet and run up and down the beach and around the flats. All paid for with cash. And out in front, some nice pickup which changed make, model and color every month or so because I totaled them with wild driving, though never in a collision with another car or person. I flipped them on the beach, on the sand fills, in the woods and one time, playing chicken with a palm tree that refused to move. There was no reason to notify my insurance company, because I just bought another pickup. For cash.

Cash was, after all, easy to get hold of. All gigs were done in cash, trading green weeds for green paper. The most difficult thing was where to stash it all.

I used epoxy slow set fiberglass on all my PVC pipes, plastic coolers and tackle boxes in which I buried money. First I put the money in bags, then wrapped each stack with a roll or two of duct tape that were brushed with epoxy. When dry, the stacks were now blocks of fiberglass. I lay them neatly in a cooler or whatever container

I was using. I mixed up a gallon of epoxy with a gallon of hardener and filled the cooler up until the stacks began to float in the epoxy. I weighed them down with bricks or dumbbells. When dry, I filled the other half of the cooler completely to the top. I now had the money tightly fiber-glassed inside my container. The cooler was put in a cardboard box a half-an-inch or so larger. Holding the handle up, I filled the remaining space with more epoxy. When that last step was finished and completely dry, I peeled off the cardboard and was left with a perfect block of fiberglass with a handle coming out on top. I could bury them in yards, mangrove swamps, and even tied them to pilings deep in the mud underwater, forming oyster bars. I never had one bill ruined and they were just as fresh and crisp as the day I put them in.

As soon as I bought this house, I sank an epoxied block of fiberglass, holding $375,000, on the outside piling of my dock after hosing out a hole in the mud. I tied the handle to the piling.

And, of course, there were women, coming and going at all hours of the day and night. In the front in my pickup and in the back on my boats. It was an open house of sex, drugs and rock 'n roll. I was 23 years old.

Some of us uneducated mullet fishermen had so much cash we thought we could do anything. Everyone had money. Family, friends, businesses. The mid-seventies was a time like no other.

One day I was at Mom's and Mike stopped by.

"Hey, Peggy. Could you do me a favor? I have some money out in the truck I need to stash somewhere for a day or two. Can you help me out?"

"Mike, you could put it in my bedroom and I'll keep an eye on it until you pick it up, but I want to let you know we don't lock the door too often around here, with the kids coming and going. Whatever you have, put it in my closet."

"Steve, give me a hand, will ya?"

"What? You got so much you need a hand bringin' it in?"

"Yeah, it'd help."

I walked out with Mike to his truck and he opened the tailgate. He pulled a big cardboard box toward us and handed it to me. It must have weighed fifty pounds.

He grabbed an army duffel bag, threw it over his shoulder, and said, "Where you want to put this stuff, Steve?"

"In my mom's closet, I guess. That's where she wants it. Shit! How much you got here?"

"Three or four million."

"No shit! What the hell are you doin' driving around with all this shit?"

"I'm not. I'm stashing it at your mom's house."

I walked into her bedroom and had to move Mom's shoes and half her wardrobe to make room for Mike's cash.

"Hang on. I've got more in the truck."

"How big is it, Mike?"

"Just like the box you carried in."

"Damn, son, that's gonna fill up most of the closet."

From that evening on, every time I stopped by Mom's, it was "Where's our friend? It's been two weeks." "It's been three weeks." "It's been a month. Steve, this is ridiculous. It's going on two months. My entire closet's full. Tell Michael to come over and get these boxes. I'm so worried I can't even sleep at night. Plus I'm working all the time and anyone could get in here."

At the same time, Barry was complaining that Mike had left a million with him—'to keep a day or two'—and it was still there, under his kitchen sink.

I continued to hassle Mike and one day he arrived, took his millions, and left.

Mike wasn't the only one who had to find a place to hide money. I did, too.

One time I sat with Sue and Pat, my sister and brother-in-law, counting twenty dollar bills into five thousand dollar stacks, wrapping them and putting them into four-foot PVC pipes, which were 18 inches in diameter. We stuffed a half a million dollars in four pipes, $125,000 each. We also counted a quarter million in hundreds I wanted to bury. I put that quarter million in a plastic tackle box, then fiberglassed it. It took us all night.

I buried them in Sue's backyard, the PVC pipes in a hole the size of a small grave, right behind the porch; the tackle box in a far corner.

I felt good leaving it there because Sue and Pat had a privacy fence, unlike Mom's place where the backyard was open to all the neighbors. Every time I buried money in her yard, I brought her a bush or a small palm to plant over it. It began to look like a jungle.

We lived, loved and enjoyed the luxuries of that blessed time of "No problem, mon," when every minute and breath was joyous, exciting, vibrant, and spiritually electrifying. It was a rush of thanksgiving and happiness.

I was getting high every day.

"Hey, Steve. Are we gonna check the shark lines in the morning?"

"Hell, I pulled an all-nighter. I wanna get some sleep right now, Castle. Won't feel like messin' with sharks in the morning."

"So what are you saying? We're not gonna set any lines today at all?"

"Jimmy! It's Ladies' Night at the Crown Lounge. I'll be on my two-to-two schedule today—wake up at two in the afternoon and close the clubs at two in the morning. And then there's sexercising 'til daybreak. I surely won't feel like dancing with any eight-foot bull sharks. Not after Ladies' Night, Jimmy. We'll set some tomorrow."

Every day, including the days I worked at the Aquatarium, I rolled out of bed, did a little bump, and rolled a joint—all before I shit, showered and shaved—then rolled a handful of thumb-sized joints to carry with me, knowing that most of my co-workers enjoyed burning Gold Bud throughout the day.

We could smoke joints and still work perfectly, undetected by those who were not indulging. After a nice big, fat, Gold Bud I could do everything better, and it made everything I was doing so much more enjoyable. It wasn't like drinking alcohol, which made me off balance, loud, and slurred my words, while work would have been almost impossible. The last thing you'd want to do when working with five hundred pound cats would be unaware of what was happening around you. There was no way management wouldn't have known if I'd come in drunk. I would have been fired on the spot. Yet when high on pot, I was often complimented for the work I did.

Money and drugs flowed. There wasn't anything we couldn't do. We had life by the balls.

TWENTY-FOUR

"C'MON, SUN DOG, load up."

We headed out to the middle of Blind Pass and cruised toward the bridge in Tuna Jim's Seacraft. On board was Mammal driving, Miss Jane and Roxie sitting in the swivel seats beside him, Strings holding onto the console next to Miss Jane, and Barry sitting on the bow with his legs dangling over, his arms tight on the bow rail.

Jim was a phenomenal skier. He could do all types of tricks, on skis and off of them. I really wanted to master barefoot skiing and he was the one to teach me. When we got to the bridge, Mammal turned the boat around and headed south down the middle of the Pass where we had plenty of room. Jim and I dropped overboard with our own ski rope in hand and a slalom on one foot.

When barefooting, you have to be moving along, so we were doing close to 50 miles an hour when I dropped my ski and was doing my thing with no wood under my feet. Yeah, baby! I was barefoot skiing! But not for long. I ate shit and started bouncing and sliding across the water at 50 miles an hour.

There were five people in the boat and every one of them were looking back at Tuna walking on water or me, skipping like a flat rock beside him. When I found my shorts and came up for a gulp of air, I watched the open Sea Craft full of people speeding at an angle toward the longest dock on the point.

I was in the water no more than fifty yards north of the dock the boat was heading for. I waved my arms madly, screaming and pointing. "Hey! Look in front of you! *The fucking dock!*"

The girls waved back, laughing and pointing at me. "*NO! NO!*"

In slow motion, the boat edged toward the outside piling of the longest dock. *BoWHAM!* The piling gave way, but didn't break. The boat ran up at a 45-degree angle and went airborne like a rocket, the prop at least eight to ten feet in the air. Gas cans flew out and Sun Dog right behind them. I watched the boat glide as if I was in a deep nightmarish dream, until *SLAM!* it made perfect contact with the second dock. It landed in the middle of the dock, which broke, giving way but snapping back, as the prop bit into the wood, and launched the boat like a projectile being slung from a slingshot to the third dock, where finally, it slid to a stop.

Onlookers crowded the seawall on both sides of Blind Pass, brought out by the sounds of the crash.

I flagged down a boat heading toward the scene.

"Hey, I need a ride down to the wreck! Those are my friends."

"Climb in," one guy said, giving me a hand. "What the hell happened?"

"Two of us were skiing behind the boat and I saw it headed toward the dock. Next thing I knew it was airborne. I saw my dog fly outta the boat, but no people. God! I hope they're all right."

"We heard it from inside the apartment. Helluva noise!"

"Shit! You shoulda seen it happen. It jumped two or three docks." We arrived at the point and it looked like a war zone. Toothpick to timber-size debris floated on the surface. "Is everyone all right? Is Sun Dog okay? I saw him fly out of the boat."

"Sunny swam over to your dock," Mammal yelled. "I've got a scratch on my arm, otherwise I'm okay. The girls are all okay, too."

"Steve! Barry's not here," Strings shouted.

I dove overboard immediately, but I couldn't see an inch in front of me in the muddy water, with the tide low and running out. Strings and I dove repeatedly. I felt only flesh-cutting barnacles, sea cucumbers and other strange, slippery, squishy things knocked off the pilings by the crash.

"You find anything?" Strings shouted.

"Everything but Barry. Where did he come off the boat?"

"I don't know. We hit that outside piling first. The whole bow rail's gone. He was holdin' on to the bow rail so he must've gone with it."

"I see something shining over here," a woman on the seawall yelled, and pointed to an area about forty or fifty feet from me. I swam along the wall to where she was standing, and dove. I felt the bow rail in about three feet of water. I worked my way out deeper holding on to the mangled rail, fighting the tide, and suddenly felt a handful of hair.

The bow rail had a tight grip on Barry, wrapped up under his arms.

"Strings! I've got him!"

I swam with Barry in my arms over to the second dock that had broken in a V shape and fallen into the water at a 45-degree angle. I pulled him up on the dry part of the dock and gave him CPR. He soon began coughing up foam and beer, but he'd been down for at least ten minutes. I tried and tried, until the paramedics arrived and carried him away.

Considering his injuries, it was probably the best thing that could have happened to Barry, dying like he did on the way to Palms of Pasadena Hospital.

BARRY WAS LIKE family, and one of my best friends. I didn't know what to do, but I did know I was going to give him a funeral and somehow try to get in touch with his family. Barry hadn't seen his father in a long time and I didn't know how to reach him, until I found Barry's older brother, Jeff, who said he'd notify their father.

I told him I'd fly them down here and back, and put them up at a hotel on the beach.

We had dinners together, luncheons together; talked of Barry and their times of growing up. It was a time of bonding with his father, although posthumously.

Bob Harper, Funeral Director of the St. Petersburg Beach Memorial, lived on the next block over, and I asked him to take care of the funeral. "I don't care what it costs; make it nice for Barry." I picked out the most comfortable looking coffin of those he showed me.

I then made arrangements with the pastor of the Pass-A-Grille Church, across from Hurley's Little League baseball field, to conduct the service at the funeral home.

I chartered Wilson Hubbard's largest fishing vessel, the *Florida Fisherman,* to carry his friends and take Barry's body offshore at least nine miles out, as the law required. I would then have Wilson line up the boat with Eighth Street off Pass-A-Grille Beach, Barry's stomping grounds.

THE FUNERAL PARLOR was packed with people, having more of a party than a funeral. Barry would have wanted it that way. He always had a smile—he didn't know how to frown—and he still had that smile when he was in his casket, all decked out in a nice new suit.

There were so many flowers around his coffin they spilled out into the main parlor. Barry had friends! His father, sitting beside me, broke into tears. "Steve, this is a really lovely thing you have done for Barry. I never realized he was loved by so many people."

"Mr. Korn, Barry was one in a million. He was everyone's friend."

The room may have been stacked with flowers, but that eternal resting spot of his was lined with his friends' version of heavenly happiness—drugs. It seemed as if every other person who passed by his coffin slipped in something: a picture, a joint or two, fat homegrown buds, Thai sticks. There were fat joints in his hands, his fingers, his pockets, and along and under the pillow his head rested on, Quaaludes and pills of every color and size. Everywhere drugs could be laid, drugs were laid. He had quite a stash to take with him offshore to Davy Jones' locker. He would definitely rest in peace.

After the service, people filled Corey Avenue, waiting to follow the hearse to Hubbard's Pier.

In the meantime, Gary King, Buddy Gilkes, and I had a little modification to make to Barry's casket.

Bob Harper wheeled the coffin into a back room and we followed.

"Okay, boys," he said, "will this work?"

"Perfect. Can we use this door to the parking lot? Buddy's donating the lead line he's cut off his pompano net. Should be close to two hundred pounds. You think that's enough to sink the casket?"

"Ought to be, but you're going to need some holes in the casket or it might float, even with that much weight."

"No problem. Gary's got a drill out in his truck. Anything else we need?"

"Then I think you've got it well taken care of. Let me know if there's anything I can help you with. I'll have the hearse ready when you're finished."

In the parking lot Gary retrieved his tools. Buddy and I dragged in three five-gallon buckets filled to the rim with three-inch leads from his net, closed and locked the door behind us.

I opened the lid to the casket. "Hey, Barry, I hate to bother you, but we're gonna have to slide you out of here for just a couple minutes. Don't worry, I'll make sure we get all your stash back in the coffin so you can make a fine impression on Davey Jones. Although I wouldn't mind borrowing a Quaalude or two of yours while we're doing this.

"C'mon guys, let's get Barry out of this coffin." I slid my hands under his shoulders. He felt rock hard, like a stuffed marlin. "C'mon, help me."

"This is gonna be weird," Buddy said. "You sure he's not gonna break up?"

"I hope not. Mr. Harper said he's intact. Shit! His coat's not. It's comin' off. The back's completely open."

"Don't worry; that's how they dress corpses," Gary said.

"Well, hell, do they have underwear and pants on 'em?"

"Yeah, we're all right on this end," Buddy said as he lifted up Barry's legs.

We carried Barry over to a big leather chair and leaned him up against it. He started to slide down, and we put him back.

"Hell, Barry, stay put."

I let go and he started sliding again. "Here, bring that little table over and put it against him next to the chair. There you go, Barry. How's that?"

Barry gave me no answer nor expression—other than that nice smile of his. Who wouldn't be smiling, covered with all the pot buds and Thai sticks and finger fat-size joints sticking out of his pockets and between his fingers as far as they'd go. He would have loved it.

"Let's put some holes in this coffin and get this job done," Gary said. "Lamb, you ain't right, sitting there carrying on a conversation with Barry as if he could hear ya. You're damn strange." He turned on his drill.

"Wait a minute, Gary. Lemme get some of that loose stash out before you rip it all up."

I gathered Barry's gifts as fast as I could and put them in a pile on the table that was keeping him against the leather chair.

"Don't worry, Barry. You'll have all your stash—minus a Quaalude or two. Damn, Gary. You drillin' right through all the satin? I shoulda' bought a cheaper casket. He sold me on all the soft, silky stuff which you're tearing holes right through."

"Damn, Lamb. The whole coffin's lined with this stuff. It's messin' up my drill. Quit bitchin' about the friggin' coffin."

"Barry, look what he's doin' to your bed."

"Lamb, will you stop talking to Barry and give Buddy a hand with the fuckin' leads!"

"Shit, Gary, he's got to live there the rest of his life, or whatever. Damn, Barry, he's tearing up your house. At least you'll have a holey house. God bless you, Bro."

We poured buckets of lead in poor Barry's torn-up silky bed. I pulled the table away from Barry and he thought he was going places. I caught him before he slid to the floor. "Buddy, give me a hand with him. Gary, that's probably enough damn holes. You drillin' the roof, too?"

"The last thing we want is Barry floating around out in the middle of the Gulf. Gotta be sure he's goin' straight down."

We laid him back into his coffin. I gave him a peck on the cheek. "I'll get a Loran reading when we drop you,

Barry, so I'll know your new address. I'll stop by some-time when I'm diving."

We filled his coffin back with his eternal gifts. Before closing the top we gave him one last look. There he was, resting on that pillow—the only thing left untouched by Gary's drill—covered with his drugs and pictures of friends. He reminded me of an Egyptian king with all his gifts for his afterlife. His pyramid would be the entire Gulf of Mexico.

We walked with Mr. Harper and his associate as they wheeled the casket to the hearse. As Mr. Harper opened the back door, his helper pushed the casket inside.

"This is your last car ride, Barry. I'm taking you down to Pass-A-Grille for a boat ride. Then you're going swimming."

"Lamb," Gary whispered in my ear with clenched teeth. "Shut the hell up. He's dead. Quit talkin' to Barry. *He's dead!*"

Buddy tapped me on the shoulder. "Steve, he's right. It's time to say goodbye to Barry. Let him rest in peace."

"What do you think I'm doing, Buddy? I'm tellin' him goodbye. I'm just telling him where he's goin' right now."

"Damn, Lamb, what did you do? Get into Barry's stash?"

"He told me to take a couple Quaaludes with me."

Everyone was finally in their cars and heading south to Pass-A-Grille down Gulf Boulevard. The mile-long line of traffic had a police escort. Smaller boats filled with friends dotted the bay. The *Florida Fisherman* was packed to its max as we left the dock. The pastor went with us and said a few words. We all prayed a blessed farewell and the coffin and flowers slid overboard. And damn, in spite of all those holes, Barry insisted on floating around.

The coffin took a good four or five minutes to fill up with water before all that was left was a garden of float-ing flowers.

Barry was gone, but not forgotten.

TWENTY-FIVE

I BECAME FRIENDS with Steve and Danny, the two brothers who picked me up in the middle of the pass when Barry was killed. Steve was the manager of an apartment building on Blind Pass, a couple of blocks down the street from my house. They had a little boat and enjoyed fishing, so we had lots to talk about.

When they found out I was one of the Steinhatchee Seven, we had a lot more to talk about.

As we became good friends and neighbors, I loaded the brothers with ten thousand pounds of Colombian Gold Bud that they took to Michigan. *Michigan.* What a small world. We knew many of the same people.

I fronted those ten thousand pounds at $250 a pound. They sold it for $300 a pound, making a quick half a million dollars middling the product.

They returned a week later with two and a half million dollars, which was owed for the front. (The middleman always takes the Franklins, the hundreds, because they stack much nicer and in smaller packages than tens and twenties, plus weigh less.)

The money I was receiving was called "street money" because it is mainly tens and twenties, the bills one mainly sees on the streets in everyday business affairs. With the boxes, army duffel bags and stacks of money came a handful of fifties and hundreds. But it was mainly $10 and $20 U.S. bills.

A bill weighs right at a gram. That means if I have $100,000 in $100 bills, the weight is very close to 1,000 grams, which is a kilogram. A kilo in pounds is 2.2046 pounds. Let's say 2.2 pounds. If you multiply that $100,000 by 10, you would have 22 pounds of $100 bills to make a million dollars. A million in $20s weighs 110 pounds; one million in $10 bills weighs 220 pounds. Two-and-a-half million dollars starts getting pretty heavy if it's in tens and twenties. Yes, it is heavy, and it is also pretty.

"Seein' I have two and a half million in mostly tens and twenties, there's over two hundred pounds of weight in these duffel bags and boxes. Grab hold and help me drag 'em downstairs to my truck."

As I started loading Steve on a regular basis, he offered me an apartment in his building that I could use as a stash place. It turned out to be a nice set-up. I had murals of tropical scenes of toucans in banana trees, white sandy beach with shrimp boats coming into a blue water bay. It worked great as my secret spot to hide from the open-door policy I had at my house. And for certain women.

One day Steve asked if I could get him a skiff quick. He had a gig coming in in two nights. Four thousand pounds. He wanted to unload off of Blind Pass; could I help him?

I knew of a skiff in Pass-A-Grille he could get for ten thousand dollars.

Would I lend him the money? He'd pay me back the next day.

So I helped him out.

A week and a half passed. No Steve, No money.

In the meantime, Big John Parker, a friend of mine who lived in Gulfport, asked if I could move four thousand pounds for a guy he knew.

"It's up in Tennessee," he said.

"What's the ticket on it?"

"I'm not sure. He was the captain, and I think he stole the load. He just off-loaded the four thousand himself with a couple of other guys and took it up to Tennessee. He needs somebody to move it and he asked me."

"Naw, I don't need the karma moving a load of stolen pot. What's the story on it?"

"Apparently they were goin' to unload off of Blind Pass, but he took it up to the Panhandle and off-loaded it himself."

"That's strange, Big John. I know someone else who was doing four thousand. I don't want to get involved. Doesn't sound right."

I finally went over to Steve's apartment and confronted him and asked about my $10,000.

"They had a problem. Had to scuttle the whole load."

"Someone just offered me four thousand pounds that they have stashed north of here and were supposed to off-load it a week or so ago off of Blind Pass. You sure the captain didn't beat you?"

"Oh, no. I dove on the boat. It was full of bales. I saw 'em."

"That's bullshit. You got beat. What's with my money? You just planning on goin' out the Pass every day with your girl friend, riding right past me with all your dive gear and fishing poles on board and never stopping by and I've got to come beg for my money?"

And I thought I was getting a deal with a free apartment. Guess everything costs you something.

Crab Traps . . .

load
bait
wait

Crab Claws . . .

catch
heat
eat

TWENTY-SIX

IN SPITE OF having all the money I needed, I still enjoyed doing things I loved with friends, like fishing and crabbing. Hell, even working at the Aquatarium was joyous because I loved being around the fish and the animals. I cooked up fresh stone crabs in beer on almost a daily basis at The Oyster Shucker on Blind Pass, where they served fresh seafood, and smoked mullet. I loved stone crabbing for Verne and Leta, the owners.

And I loved spending time there, too. We had open-garden concerts there. Harry Daily, Jimmy Buffet's bass player lived in one of the three apartments in the back at the restaurant. With hundreds of kids listening to music, drinking beer, and getting high, it was easy for me to find the numbers I needed for yet another venture.

Friends and I invested in many different exciting adventures which always became more adventure than profit. Although the lawyers always seemed to come out ahead. There was Road Atlanta and Watkins Glen, New York. At the Glen I had a helicopter and pilot that came along with the deal to watch the race from above. The pilot freaked out when I told him I wasn't interested in watching a bunch of cars go around a track. I wanted to see deer. "I'll tip you a hundred for every one we see," I told him.

I didn't know New York had so many deer. I had a blast zipping over the trees and down into the fields, all the while peeling off Franklins for the pilot. With money you can do things in life that are just impossible to do without money.

At car races, I was right there as drivers pulled in the pits; at concerts I was backstage. When Jimmy Buffett received a platinum record of one of his hits and a thank-you dinner for his benefit concerts during Jimmy Carter's campaign, we all stayed at the Watergate Hotel in Washington, D.C.

Close friends hired Jimmy Buffett to put on a concert on the Tom Sawyer out of St. Petersburg for some of their beach friends.

One of my Michigan buyers was close friends with the Rolling Stones, and I went to a number of their concerts and backstage with them. At one party after a concert in Florida, I was more than glad to give a set of shark jaws that were in my pickup truck to Keith Richards. I wished I'd had more jagged-tooth gifts to give the whole security crew of the Stones who seemed to really like them.

The more money a person has, the more friends he has.

In the meantime, the garage apartment at my house on Sunset Beach was remodeled into a gym filled with free weights. In fact, half of my garage apartment had been welded into dip bars, pull-down bars, squat racks. The place turned into pig iron. Some friends I worked with at the Aquatarium liked using the gym and I was also pumping some weight myself, so I had no problem with them coming over often.

However, with their vehicles—everyone working, living and affiliated with the Aquatarium drove big black cars and trucks—being parked in front of my house on a daily basis, the place looked like a gathering place for organized crime.

These guys were body builders, veterinarians, marine biologists and at times, marine patrol officers. All good, honest guys. But with my recent bust in Steinhatchee and my other friends and the partying I was doing, and with boats pulling up to my dock all day long and into the night, plus those big black Cadillacs and trucks parked out front every day, maybe it wasn't such a good idea.

Early one morning the phone rang.

"You still in bed?" an unrecognized voice asked. "It's almost seven o'clock. You should be up and at 'em."

"Who's this?"

"You don't know me, but I know you. I know who you are and I know what you do. And I really like that house you're in."

Try as I could, I couldn't recognize the voice. "Who is this? Hello. Hello."

Click.

Now I was awake. Who in the hell was that? I didn't like the vibes I got off that phone call. Something was weird.

All day I tried to figure out that phone call. Had I ever heard that voice before? I kept getting bad feelings from just the way he talked.

Later that afternoon, as soon as I got in the house, the phone rang.

"Shouldn't stay out in that boat so long," the suddenly familiar voice said. "You could get burned. And who was the good-looking, big-breasted blond you were sittin' next to at the Seahorse? You called her Diesel. Is that her real name?"

Click.

Who the hell? I was back at the Seahorse. Who the hell was sitting right around DeeDee and me? I tried to remember. Faces. Voices. The place was packed. Everyone was playing foosball. Every seat taken. Who was sitting by us? They had to follow me in the boat. I didn't *see* anybody. Then be sitting alongside us. *Who was there?*

My mind danced around the rest of the day. I was just getting ready to go out to the Crown Lounge when the phone rang again.

"What's up? You gettin' ready to go out?"

Click.

I was awakened again the following morning. This went on for the next few weeks. A voice telling me where I went, what I ate, who I was with. I was now observing everyone who followed me in my truck, passed me in the boat, or sitting anywhere near me when I was anyplace at all. I was aware of everyone, everywhere.

Where are you, motherfucker! Who are you?

One day when I returned home, at least one of my questions was answered. Peanut, my girlfriend, and a partner of mine, Bert, were waiting for me. They had met the mysterious phone caller.

"Oh, Steve, I'm so glad you're home. Three guys were here." Peanut could hardly talk.

"Shit, Lamb," Bert said. "They had vice grips on my nuts. And a gun in my ear. They thought I was you."

"Wait a minute. *What?*"

"I heard a knock," Peanut said, still shaking. "When I went to answer, a guy came flyin' in with a gun in his hand. Two others behind him. They made me call to find you. I called Bert's—"

"Yeah, I came right over because she said she was havin' a problem. They grabbed me as soon as I came in."

"Calm down, Peanut. I'm here now. You're okay."

"He slammed me in the chest with the gun and knocked me on the floor. He put thumb cuffs on me."

"Whatta you mean *thumb* cuffs?"

"The cops use 'em, Steve," Bert answered for her. "Just like handcuffs, but they fit over your thumbs."

"What the hell did they want?"

"They were goin' to pop my nuts if I didn't tell 'em where the money was buried."

"What money? What the fuck are they talkin' about?"

"They said they had a bug in an air conditioner duct right next to where you were runnin' your jaw. About how much money weighs when you were pickin' up two and a half million dollars at Steve's apartment."

"But I don't—"

"Lemme finish. Said you told Steve that the captain on his boat stole the four thousand pounds he was supposed to get. He doesn't even know what you look like, but he knows you picked up two and a half million a while back and he wants it. Where did you have it buried? Like I would know!"

I didn't know what to say to Peanut or Bert for all they'd been through. I knew it was my fault that this happened.

Yet calling the police didn't seem the thing to do. Neither Bert nor I were in a position to be explaining anything about money to them.

The next morning the phone rang.

"Stopped by to see you yesterday, but I missed you. Cute little girl friend you have. Your neighbor almost shit himself when I had his balls in that vice grip."

"Listen, buddy. I—"

"I'm not your buddy. I'm your worst fuckin' nightmare. You better grab the shovel and start diggin' 'cause some of that money's got my name on it."

"I don't know what—"

Click.

Every time the phone rang I froze. Just the sound scared the hell out of me. I felt like ripping it out of the wall. I started meeting Peanut over at her house a lot more.

The calls came more often and were more descriptive, telling me everything I did during the day and sometimes the night. And then one night, another break-in.

Again, Peanut was home and I wasn't. Again, she was cuffed and threatened, although this time they didn't wear masks. The three guys waited in my living room for hours, asking repeatedly, "Where is he?" "When's he comin' home?"

Tough little Peanut stared them down with the same answer: "I have no idea." Finally, they left, letting her know they'd be back again and wouldn't stop coming by until they found me.

This is bullshit! I don't know who the guys are, but it was time to call the police.

We went to the police station and Peanut gave a description of the three men and hoped for the best.

One night after net fishing with Mark Knight, Mike's little brother, we pulled up to my dock. The lights were still on in the house, which meant Peanut was still up. Damn! I wanted to go to the Gallery.

"We've still got time to make last call," Mark said.

"Yeah. Let's take the boat to the Oyster Shucker," I suggested, "tie it up and we'll walk down to the Gallery. If I go in the house now I'm stuck. Peanut's not going for that last-call bullshit. It's best I don't even go in. Let's just cruise down the pass."

That decision saved my ass, or my nuts, if he had his vice grips with him. When I did get home, I learned there'd been the three of them heavily armed, waiting for my arrival until almost daybreak. They left just before I walked in the door.

His next call threatened my youngest sister. "It's time to get serious, Lamb. You're gonna get me a hundred thousand dollars or I'll send your little sister's ear in the mail. Think that's worth a hundred grand? Be a shame to hit her on that brand new little yellow moped you just bought her. Think about it."

Click.

This shit's got to stop! I don't even know who the fuckers are and they know all about me and my family.

I contacted my good friend Dick Price, a private investigator, and asked if he'd get something on these guys.

Once he was hired, I felt somewhat relieved, even if the phone calls didn't stop. Every day, another call. Another threat. It was getting so I was looking over my shoulder all the time. The caller knew more about what I was doing than I did.

He was like a shadow on a moonless night—not there, but always with me.

I called Dick Price again. "Dick, I've got to do something about this guy callin' me every day. He's driving me nuts. I've got to know who he is and where he's callin' from. He knows every thing I do. Every person I'm with. And he's not calling anyone else. I'm the only one he wants."

"Well, Steve, I've been right there with you in traffic on a lot of occasions and haven't picked up anybody tailing you. Been keeping an eye on your neighborhood. Nothing out of the norm there."

"You guys don't have any kind of a machine or tracking device that I can tell where these calls are comin' from? Don't you have any contacts in the phone company?"

"I actually have something better than that if I can get it. I have some friends in Washington who might be able to help us. Let me get back to you."

I hoped his 'getting back' would be soon.

It was. Within a few days Dick said he had to go to Washington to pick up a sophisticated telephone tracing machine that would give us the number and location, as well as the name of the owner of the phone if he was calling from a residence, or the location of a pay phone.

A few days later we set the machine up connected to the phone in my bedroom. I kept it covered with a fish box, keeping it as inconspicuous as a fish box in a bedroom would be. Every time I got a call, the machine spit out a paper tape listing the time, date and location.

And then he called.

And then he called again. And again. All the same day. And that's all it took.

Although it was dark, I didn't wait until morning to find where he lived.

I drove to the address off of 66th Street and found he lived in a trailer. I had his trailer and him located. His name was Gene Coats.

Now that I had the information, what was I going to do with it? I sure as hell didn't call him back.

But I did call Dick.

"Price, I found him. His name is Gene Coats and he lives off of Sixty-Sixth Street. I drove out there last night. Can you do somethin' now?"

"Slow down a little bit. We need to find out that it's the right person. Phone could just be listed in Coats' name. Doesn't mean he's the one making the calls, or even that your caller lives there, you know. Just hold tight."

"Hold tight? Shit! How long?"

"Let me check a few things. I'll get back to you as soon as I can."

The next day I jumped into my pickup with Tom Byerly, and headed over the Skyway Bridge toward Cortez, carrying a load of mullet. The Chevy had a herd of ponies under the hood and ran a good 125-135 mph. We had the pedal to the metal and were coming down the backside of the bridge, doing close to 140.

"Damn, Lamb, you're goin' to blow 'er up if you don't ease back on her a little bit. Check that temperature gauge."

The Burliness was right. I was definitely running that engine a little too hard.

"Hey, 'Ness. I'll pull in that Shell Station right over the bridge."

I needed to get a little gas, anyway, and pulled into the gas station in Terra Ceia, jumped out, and popped the hood.

"Fill 'er up, Cap," I told the little hillbilly of a dude who came out of the station. "I'm gonna get a little water, too."

"It's over there in the red bucket, Sir."

"No hose?"

"No, Sir. We just have the spigot."

"Thank you, pardner. I'll take care of the water, you just fill 'er up back there."

I put the bucket down and covered the radiator cap with a rag and let the steam off slowly. I glanced over at the battery.

"Fuck! Look at this, 'Ness. What the hell is this, Christmas?"

Three wires, red, green and black, ran from a PVC pipe to the number one spark plug, my starter, and the battery. The pipe had been cut into by the alternator belt, and white foam was bubbling from the gash.

"What the hell kind of rig you got hooked up to your motor? What's with the PVC pipe?"

"It's a fuckin' bomb! How the hell did he put that in here. He had to be right in my front yard."

"You know who the guy is?"

"A bomb?" the little hillbilly yelled. "Get that thing the hell out of my gas station."

"Steve! Whatcha gonna' do?"

241

I grabbed my shucking gloves from the back of the truck and put them on, undid the wires, and carefully eased the PVC out as it continued to bubble.

Byerly looked at the pipe in my hands. "You really know who did this?"

"Pretty sure. Just found out his name last night."

"You need to take him on a long walk off a short pier. Can't be—"

"*Sir!* Would you please get this truck away from these gas pumps and off of this property?"

"Want me to pay you, or what?"

"Just get that damn thing outta here!"

"Pardner, take this and keep the change for your trouble," I said, handing him a hundred.

I put the PVC in the back with the mullet and continued to the fish house in Cortez. I called Dick Price from a pay phone at the fish house.

"Dick! The sonofabitch put a bomb in my truck! A fuckin' bomb! He—"

"Slow down, Stevie. Let me—"

"I just found it! Pulled in to put some water in the radiator and there it was! He wants to kill me!"

"You sure it's a bomb?"

"Fuckin' A, it's a bomb! It's a pipe bomb. Piece of PVC foaming at the top with wires hanging all over."

"Here's what you do, Steve. You go right to the Treasure Island Police Department and give it to them. Don't mess with it at all. Take it directly to the cops and let them handle it."

"Should I call that detective, Everett Rice? He was the one who investigated that break-in when they tied Peanut up. He seemed like a good guy and really wanted to get those guys."

"He's with the Sheriff's Department. I think you should just turn it over to your local cops. They'll call him if necessary."

242

I drove straight there. Boy, did the questions start. I knew nothing and said nothing.

The next morning, the phone rang.

"What's up, friend? You sleeping in? You're burnin' daylight—" my hand shook as I listened. I could hardly breathe, much less answer the voice. "We're such good friends talking on the phone every day like this, ear to ear, I can't wait until we meet eye to eye."

Even though I now knew who he was after all these months, thinking about being face to face with that voice scared the shit out of me. I just listened because I sure as hell couldn't talk.

"Friend, before you go rushin' out to your truck to jump in and drive off to enjoy your day, I would suggest you look under the hood and see what I left you for Christmas." He chuckled, but it sure wasn't Santa. I was too scared to tell him I'd already found it. What if it pissed him off? Who knew what he'd do next?

"I put just enough to blow the hood through the windshield. Give you some nice memories. Not enough to kill you. Lots of publicity for your sorry ass.

"What? Cat's got your tongue. Can't say nothin' Lamb?"

I couldn't fuckin' talk and he knew it. I was scared as a rabbit in a python's cage.

"I hear you breathin' Lamb, so I know you're there. And you're still listening. I'll be seein' you soon. Can't wait to get with ya."

Click.

A knock at the door made me jump a foot off my bed. I crept to the bathroom window and looked out. Thank God! It was Mike Knight!

"Lamb! You look like a ghost. What the hell's goin' on?"

"Shit! I just got off the phone with that fucker who calls me every day."

243

"What's this stuff Byerly told me about you guys findin' a bomb?"

"That's the guy! He just called me. His name is Gene Coats. Lives off of Sixty-Sixth Street. He didn't know I found it. Told me to take a look under the hood. Scared to tell the sonofabitch I'd already found it. You never got any calls did ya?"

"He'd never fuck with me. I'm affiliated with friends of John Carroll's, who have fingers the size of cigars. He knows better. What are you gonna do?"

"I'm calling Posey."

TWENTY-SEVEN

"ALL THIS SHIT'S from a damn bug in an air conditioner, Posey."

"I'll be down. We'll take care of the damn varmint."

Posey, who held all my drugs in the warden's office for me when I was in federal prison, came down. Posey and his crew were my main unloading boys. They were all strictly hilligans from Lookout Mountain and were some serious players. People I could count on.

In spite of being scared to death, I partied even more, maybe, *because* of being scared to death.

Mike Ogden, Miguelito, one of my captains and crew members on trips in the past, stayed at my house much of the time. I felt better having him around with Coats still out there looking for me.

Right then Miguelito got involved in a thirty-thousand-pound gig in Louisiana and was busted along with the others on the boat. When he got back after bonding out, he said, "I'll be damned if I'm going to court, Lamb. I'm heading to Venezuela."

He left to stay with three Venezuelan brothers who had gone to college with him in Gainesville. I told him I'd help him out financially.

Posey and I went to Coats' trailer—and got run off by his guard dog—so I never got a chance to see him. Posey and his boys, however, later had an eye-to-eye conversation with the fine, fine fellow and apparently they came to quite an understanding. The next day was the first day there were no calls from Coats.

NEW FRIENDS SOON became old friends, and all night parties continued to be the norm. Among the new ones who were fast becoming good buddies, were Gail and her two big bodybuilding guys who moved in across the street.

Loads came and went, as did the money. We were burying it all over the area, so we'd have it there when we needed it. I figured I'd soon be able to stop smuggling and get into some legal businesses I enjoyed. A fish house or a surf shop—anything to do with the ocean. I always loved hunting, too. It would be nice to have a hunting camp someplace in the Rockies. Find a house somewhere in the islands for my mother. It was always her dream to go to an island, any island. We lived on one, of course, St. Pete Beach, but I'm not talking about that one. Something more exotic and tropical. Yeah, she'd love that.

One day when Rusty Ercious and I were in my little mullet boat, the Tremblay, running along the beach looking for fish, I saw the spray from Mike's custom-built thirty-five foot Smiley boat. I loved his boat and went down to Bradenton when it was being built. I even painted the smiley face on the stern, just like the one I tattooed on my leg in prison. From then on, everyone called it the Smiley Boat.

I was going to have one built just like it, but two feet longer and with a fourteen-foot beam. In fact, two days earlier, I'd dropped off seventy grand in hundred dollar bills to Steve Davis, the boat builder.

Mike pulled up to us. "Let Rusty take your boat in. Get in with me. I need to talk to you, Steve."

Mike had that look on his face. I climbed up on the Smiley, and the big Detroit 892 double turbines started singing as we headed offshore toward the south, throwing lips of water off the bow.

We were offshore Bunces Pass a couple of miles when he pulled back on her. "I just wanted to get offshore a ways where nobody would hear us."

"Shit, Mike. They got pretty good ears if they're listening to us out here. What's up with all the gas jugs in the boat? Damn gas. Boat smells of gas. What's up, Mike?"

"That fucking Coats. I'll use him for bait, that son of a bitch."

"Slow down, son. What's up?"

"I had the Smiley tied off at the Seventh Street Pier for the night and he plugged up my scupper holes and poured ten or fifteen gallons of gas all over the floor and put twelve to fifteen milk jugs filled with gas in the nets, in the forward cabin. He wanted to blow my boat up! I found two full packs of matches with cigarettes behind 'em. He expected the cigarettes to burn down and set the matches off. That'd set off the gas. A boat must've come by and thrown a wake. Lucky for me, the gas rolled up on the cigarettes and put 'em out. He wanted to blow my fucking boat up like a stick of dynamite! What are we gonna do with this fella, Steve? We gotta do something about this Coats guy."

That was the first time Gene Coats started messing with any other smugglers. Now the mad wolf was out among the herd.

Not too long after Mike's boat incident, Strings returned from Burr Louis's house in Cortez where Burr had loaded him up with a cooler full of stone crab claws. He called up to his girlfriend to give him a hand with the heavy cooler.

She didn't answer, so he entered his apartment. Someone stuck a shotgun straight into his face and demanded money. His girlfriend had been tied up and held hostage while they waited for him.

"We'll blow her head off if you don't start coming up with some money, buddy."

"I've got fifty thousand under my spare tire."

They took that and left. Now Strings had met the wolves.

In spite of the fear Coats was spreading around, parties at the house got better and better. More and more people passed through the doors and more and more women through my bedroom. Sunset Beach was one big block party. What a life I had!

"Martie, I got a cookout at the end of the week. I want to put new carpet in the house. You interested?"

"Yeah, I can be over there Thursday or Friday."

"No, I'm talkin' about today."

"There's no way I could do it today. I'm jammed up 'til the end of the week."

"I got a fifty pound bale of Gold Bud in the gym in the garage. Give you as much as you can cram in a grocery bag if you can get here today."

"I'll be over in an hour."

And so it went. I had a twelve hundred pound stash of Colombian gold blocks stashed at my sister's mother-in-law's ranch in Seminole that was for partying, for getting boats, trucks, engines rebuilt, for house remodeling, and just to flat freak people out by telling them to take home as big a handful as they could grab. Colombian hash bud could get most things done quicker than money.

My house was like the Welcome Wagon. I loved turning my neighbors on to good buds, fresh fish and stone crabs. It was a helluva friend-maker.

One day after working out in the garage, we walked out to the driveway.

"Check it out. There's a big-ass camera lens in the window," Big Jim said, pointing to the apartment across the street where Gail and her two buddies lived.

"What? Where?"

"That top window. Right up there."

"No way. Those are friends of mine. They've been livin' there for months. They're from up north."

Byerly squinted in the direction. "I don't see nothin' up there, Maslanka."

"I'm telling you, I saw a camera. Someone was taking pictures of us standing out here."

"Bullshit."

"I'm tellin' you, *I SAW A CAMERA!*"

"Paper Ass, you'd better leave that toot alone. You're getting' paranoid."

"Shittin' me. There was a camera over there. Go over and check it out."

"That's just what I'll do."

I walked over and up the steps, and knocked on Door 54. Gail opened it.

"Hey, Steve. What's up?"

"I'm just checking. A buddy of mine said he saw a camera in your window pointed down at us."

"A camera? Here? Why would we have a camera?"

"I don't know. He's just paranoid. Did a couple of lines, been working out hard, probably seeing things. You guys want a bump?"

"Sure, I'd love one, but we're cooking dinner right now. Don't want to spoil my supper. Could I get some for after dinner?"

"Sure. Here you go. Just take what's left in the bag. And here's a couple fat spliffs of Gold Bud for you, too. Enjoy your dinner." I started down the steps, but turned back. "Hey, Gail, I caught a couple nice snook. You want a couple fillets for dinner?"

"No, we've still got a bunch of fish left from what you gave us the other day."

I went back and assured Maslanka he was seeing things.

One day a dark Latin with an accent arrived at my front door. He introduced himself as a friend of Jorge's and was here to see me about Miguelito.

"How's he doin' down there," I asked. "Does he need anything?"

"He could use a little money. And information on his case."

"Well, I know they're goin' to trial pretty soon and there's no prison time being talked about. The lawyers are working out a fine for all the defendants to pay for a library or something that they need up in Louisiana. They're more interested in the money than the jail time. Give me a number where I can contact you."

He stayed with me a couple of days, and I took him out fishing, crabbing and got him laid. It wasn't long after he went back to Venezuela that I was able to call and let him know that Miguelito's case had been taken care of with a fine and he was free to come home.

That October I was driving with my brother-in-law to see Adam, my sister's first baby. We were smoking a joint when a car came up alongside us and edged toward us.

"What's with these guys in the Grand Prix?" Pat asked, dodging the car. "They're trying to run me off the road!"

I immediately saw the wallet with a shiny badge slammed up against the window.

"Pull over!" I yelled. "They're cops."

They cut us off into a McDonald's and jumped out with guns. *These don't look like cops! Is it Coats and some of his boys?*

But then I got a closer look. It was two of my neighbors, the guys that lived with Gail.

"We're just doing our job as you were doing yours," one of them said as he was putting the containment bracelets on me. "You're really a very good person, Steve. We just walk on different sides of the fence. We could've busted you six months ago."

I was busted on delivery of a controlled substance—the bump and the two joints I gave Gail that day I was showing Maslanka he was paranoid.

Denny Caughey, my long-time friend who bonded me out in Dixie County on the Steinhatchee bust, now bonded me out on a $40,000 bond; a much smaller bond than last time, but still a serious matter.

My court date was set for January of '78. Jimmy Russell, the State's Attorney, wanted information or was talking ten years.

Hell, I wasn't going to talk, and I was just in federal prison less than five years ago. I'm sure as hell not going back. The fast lane on my highway of life was coming to a fork in the road. Now I was really thinking about how Miguelito lived as a fugitive in South America.

What's it like? Are the women pretty? I know the pot and coke is some of the best in the world. Do I have to speak Spanish? Damn! All I know are a few curse words—*Mama arrugas del mis cajonas*—where in hell can I use that? The whorehouse? Can't be starting out that way. How's the surf? Fishing? Diving? Yeah! The Amazon jungle. The Amazon River. Think of the animals and critters living on that creek. Shit, I can't *wait* to talk to Miguelito.

But when Miguelito returned to the United States, he had acquired a very strange sickness that had swollen many of his joints to twice their original size. He'd been told by Ka-ping, the chief *llanero* in Los llanos at the ranch where he lived, that he'd been cursed, and that the curse was meant to kill him.

Miguelito's sister, who worked in the Blood Bank in Gainesville, had some of the best doctors in the States check her brother out. No one in the medical field knew what was wrong with him. There were times I saw Miguelito doubled over, unable to even stand up.

When Miguelito contacted a Cuban witch doctor in Key West, he was amazingly cured. The witch doctor said he'd have to send the curse back to the original person who sent it, but he had to send it back double. "It will surely kill the sender," he said.

It was amazing. Now he was completely cured. I don't know what he did, but after he returned from Key West, he stayed at my house whenever he was in St. Pete, and I'm here to testify he was healed after that visit with the witch doctor.

Once he was rid of the curse, I wasted no time in getting my long awaited answers to the questions I had about being a fugitive. Miguelito was happy to provide me with everything he experienced and the names of those he knew would be of help.

"Do it, Lamb. You'll love Venezuela. The hell with pulling the next ten years of your life in prison again. There's no extradition in Venezuela."

"Whatta you mean, no extradition? They can't come down and get me? Even if they know I'm there?"

"No, they can't. That's what it means. Plus, where we'll stash your ass they couldn't get you if they wanted to. You'll be so deep in the jungle, the only people you'll see are *llaneros* and howler monkeys."

"What about women?"

"It's the richest country in South America and—"

"What about the *women?*"

"We'll do a little partying in San Cristobal then cross the border to Cucuta in Colombia where the whole town is a whorehouse. You can buy, sell or bargain anything in Cucuta. But after that, you're gonna have to pay your dues where I paid mine, deep in the jungle. No cars. No electricity. And one female. The cook. With a dozen kids runnin' behind her."

"Damn, Ogden, is it neat down there? Would I fit in? I don't speak Spanish. What about the people, do they like Americans?"

"They love Americans. All the technology and equipment coming down to provide jobs and pump oil out of Lake Maracalbo is from America, but Jorge will have to fly you to one of his ranches until he gets your paperwork in order."

"Whatta ya mean—one female cook?"

"Don't worry, Lamb. It's you. The way you love animals and fishin', pussy will be the last thing on your mind. For a while, anyway. There are four or five different types of monkeys. Ducks and geese of all kinds. Parrots, toucans, jaguars and ocelots. Tapirs, donkey-looking critters with a nose like an elephant. Capybaras, the world's largest rodents, twenty-five foot anacondas, with rivers full of piranha and fresh water dolphin. It's you, Lamb. Believe me. I spent almost a year in the jungle without coming out."

"Yeah, look how you came home. What'd you do? Fuck around with that one cook? And get a voodoo curse put on your ass?"

"No, Steve, you'll love it. You'll have papers as a veterinarian, a permit to carry a concealed weapon, and with those blue eyes and that blond hair, you'll have more pussy than you can shake a dick at. They all want to be Americanized. Plus the *bolivar*—that's the currency there—is four point three *bolivars* to the dollar."

With all this talk about money, Miguelito reminded me he was ready to make some. "You have anything I could do for you? I've got a brand new passport."

"Yeah, in fact, I do. I'm obligated to one more gig with a conch who wants to be loaded and unloaded. The only thing, the unload is in the Panhandle."

"As long as it's not in Louisiana."

"No, it's not Louisiana. It's north Florida."

"How's the Yucatan? I hear they have a two-hundred and ten foot cutter with a helicopter aboard, sitting in the middle of the Yucatan and you're runnin' a gauntlet just to get up to the Panhandle."

"Don't worry, my buddy doesn't. He runs a ghost boat through the Yucatan. He's got a forty-seven foot lobster boat that runs thirty knots. The shrimper runs eight. When they're just south of the Yucatan, he unloads his crew onto his lobster boat, puts the shrimp boat on automatic pilot. They run ahead and wait off the Dry Tortugas until the ghost boat has made it through the gauntlet. If there is a problem, all the Coast Guard finds is a boat full of bales with a fake registration and nobody on board."

"You're shittin' me. What a neat idea."

TWENTY-EIGHT

VENEZUELA WAS SOUNDING a lot better than ten years in prison.

Four point three *bolivars* to the dollar? I have over three million in Mom's backyard, 750 grand in Sue's backyard, 375,000 tied off the end of my dock, and a couple other play boxes. A million US is 4,300,000 *bolivars*. A few million in US and I'd be a multi-millionaire down there. I decided to head south of the border, just like the Sun Dance Kid. I wanted to make sure Miguelito could set things up for me in Venezuela. I gave him five grand and asked him to talk to Jorge and his family and make sure everything was understood. I didn't want to be a surprise and have to turn around and come back with a warrant on me. "Make sure Jorge knows I'll be having money sent down once I'm secure there."

Now, where to start? The trial was coming up in a couple of months. It was time to see a lawyer. Get new passports. Make sure my bondsman was taken care of after I left. I'd rather have the feds looking for me than a bondsman and anyway, I wouldn't feel right jumping a bond. It would be bad karma.

My thoughts were split right down the center, thinking about Mom and what it would do to her, leaving my family, my country, my friends and everything that I knew, for a new life in a place I'd never been, knew no one, and didn't speak the language. It was time to talk to a lawyer.

"I'm going to need a ten thousand dollar retainer," he said, as soon as I mentioned my plans. "I'll see what I can do." He walked me to the door. "Check back with me in two weeks."

Two weeks later when we met, he told me the smartest thing I could do was leave. "You're a pirate. You're a free spirit. And you'd be happier staying that way. You already know the jailhouse is a shit hole and I believe you'd be much happier, free. They've got a good case on you."

"I appreciate your advice. It cost me ten grand."

"If your mom ever needs any legal advice or has any problems, just tell her to come see me and it's covered. There's one other thing. Don't tell me where you're going. Just step off the world. Don't tell *anyone* you're leaving— and that includes your family, although I imagine you'll probably want to tell your mother. And don't, whatever you do, give away any of your toys: your boats, your truck, or close your bank account. Leave whatever money's in there, in there. I know you don't use banks much, but don't do anything that arouses suspicion."

My lawyer's advice was given and my mind was made up. I was at Tyrone Department of Motor Vehicles getting my driver's license in a fake name with the birth certificate and social security number I bought off a friend for five thousand dollars. My next step was to send in for a passport, which he had never gotten. I'd now get one for him, with my picture on it. Our five thousand dollar agreement was that he would never apply for a passport. He was happy to agree with that.

Now it was time for the squirrel blood to run deep within my veins and remember just where I'd buried all my stashes. I started in my mother's backyard, and then along the sides of her house. By the time I finished, her poor yard looked like a war zone that had just been bombed. I did keep a few burial sites where some of her favorite bushes were growing well. No need to ruin everything for her. I stashed stacks and stacks of hundreds throughout her whole house, in the attic, under the drawers, behind the washer and dryer. Just a much easier place for her to get to when they were called for. My next chore was harder: recovering the epoxied block of $375,000 in hundreds had been tied off under my dock for quite a while. I had to dive down with a garden hose, blow away the mud, and retrieve the box that was now completely covered in oysters and barnacles and weighed well over a hundred pounds. It took me half the day to just to get it to my seawall. I took the reef over to another lawyer's house, and he suggested we carry it to yet another lawyer's, where we spent the rest of the day and well into the night, busting off pieces of underwater growth with a sledge hammer, and then the same thing through the dried epoxy, finally getting to bread-sized loaves of bills wrapped in duct tape inches thick, and then sawing our way through to nice, crisp hundreds, as fresh as the day I sank them beneath my dock.

I still had a couple holes to dig in my sister's backyard, but I would do that in a few weeks on Thanksgiving, before the family's feast of turkey.

On the way to the airport to pick up Miguelito, I kept wondering what Jorge had said. Would he and his family accept me? How much money would it take? My questions were answered as soon as Miguelito jumped into my truck.

"*Como esta, Jefe.*"

"What the hell? Talk to me in English. What happened?"

"Buddy, you can leave your English right here in Florida, because you're not goin' to be hearing much of it where you're headed."

"What? What happened? What did he say?"

"You're lucky I broke them in. They're used to having a big, light-haired, blue-eyed American around. I told 'em you had millions and I would be bringing down money once you were there."

Damn! This was going to be a change in life. I was excited, scared and . . . and . . . was I doing the right thing? It was hard to know when I didn't know, but that's what the future always is.

As soon as we got over the bridge and onto Sunset Beach, Mike Knight pulled us over in his truck.

"That sonofabitch just burned down my brand new house and all my nets," he said as he pounded craters into the hood of his pickup.

"Who burned your house? That Coats guy who was callin' Lamb every day a few months back?"

"Yeah, that's him. I'm done fuckin' around with that guy now. Somebody's got to take him out, and don't think I won't do it. Fucker tried to blow up my boat. Now he burns down my house. The hell with my house, he burned all my friggin' nets! Sonofabitch is gonna pay."

"Lamb, when's the last time he fucked with you?"

"After Posey and his buddies came down from Alabama and had an eye-to-eye understanding with him. I haven't had another phone call or heard a word from him."

"Well, you might not have heard from him, but I'm gonna have an eye-to-eye understandin' with him. He's gonna hear from me." He jumped into his truck and peeled off rubber half a block down the street.

Oh, great, don't tell me the wolves are back in action just when I'm collecting my money. Oh, dear God, please let me slip out of here safely without being robbed, shot or killed. Or any of my family hurt. "We've got to get out of here soon, Ogden. That Coats has already threatened my family. Once I leave for South America, outta sight,

258

outta mind. My family will be safe. Plus, I'm not crazy about pullin' ten years or a day in any damn zoo."

"Exactly when do you wanna go? Jorge's ready when we are."

"I'm gonna spend the holidays with my family. We'll slip out of here the first week of the new year. Just before my court date."

"Sounds good to me. Sounds like a plan."

I still had some more of my money to collect.

SHIT, I SHOULDA hit those pipes a long time ago. I'm digging a damn grave here. I'll be in hell if I don't stop soon. How deep did I put those things? I know I didn't dig this deep.

"Yeah! A beer can." I stooped and picked up a beer can wrapped in green duct tape. "You gotta be shittin' me." A chill ran up my spine. I knew that beer can wasn't mine but the duct tape was what I'd covered the caps of the PVC pipes with.

I ran into Sue's house, grabbed the phone and called her. "Sue! What time do you get off for lunch?"

"At noon, why?"

"Shit, Sue, somebody stole my money."

"What? How could they?"

"I don't know. It had to be Jeff. Or you guys. Whoever stole it drank a beer, wrapped some of the tape around the can, dropped it in the hole and filled it back up again. It had to take an hour or more to dig those pipes up and then fill the hole back up. Shit, they coulda stole that money the day after I put it in.

This whole time I thought I had a half a million right behind your fireplace and all it turned out to be is a damn fuckin' beer can! Call Pat and tell him to bring the backhoe over. We'll take out a section of fence and dig a fuckin' pool if we have to. I can't believe someone stole

that money. I can't believe it's gone!"

"PAT, IT'S GONE, buddy. This fuckin' hole's almost six feet deep.

We shoulda found it a long time ago. It's gone. C'mon. I'm gonna check the other spot where I put the quarter million in hundreds. It's a lot smaller hole."

"LOOK PAT, HERE it is. Thank God they didn't get it all. At least they left me a tip."

BACK IN THE house Pat and I sat around the table and talked about who could have done this.

"Pat, remember that money you got for me when I was in prison for a gig we'd done with some people on the outside. I told you how to fiberglass it when you visited me; to use slow set epoxy and you used medium set?"

"Yeah, what a mess that was. When you got out, we dug it up and all the bills were stuck together. Damn! You were pissed at me. You saved half of it with that lawyer, Allen Williams, didn't you?"

"Yeah, his dad put some chemicals on it and managed to separate the bills and Allen took 'em to Vegas and we got paid for the ones that had serial numbers on both sides. Saved about half. But then I had to split that shit with the lawyer. The thing is, I had to call Jeff and use his Jeep to take all that sticky, uncured fiberglass and trash out to the woods."

Pat laughed. "Yeah, Sue wasn't going to let her Mercedes get all fucked up. Even though you bought it, she wouldn't even let you use it. Shoulda bought her a pick-up."

"After that, Jeff knew I'd hidden money here, and you guys were taking care of his Lab. Who'd pay any attention to him in your backyard? It had to take a couple of hours to dig the hole, drink a beer and fill it back in. Had to be him. Or you."

"Steve. You know you can trust us."

"Yeah, if it was you guys, you woulda took it all. Had to be Jeff."

I was sick and in shock. I busted open the epoxied tackle box and got together my quarter million in hundreds and headed back to Mom's. I dropped it off with the rest of the money and then drove to Mike's house to tell him what had happened.

When it rains, it pours. I told Mike about my mishaps, and he explained he had just lost his cooler that we buried on Sawyer Key with a half a million dollars and a couple pounds of dental gold. Mike wanted to bury it on the spot a rattlesnake was sitting. I brought that snake home, put him in a parrot cage and hung him on my front door light.

"Lamb, that snake's gonna bring us bad karma, man." Mike had said. "Leave him out here in the swamp."

I should have listened to him.

TWENTY-NINE

MOM'S TURKEY'S ALWAYS been the best I've ever eaten and it didn't disappoint me this year. She knew how to get that skin dark, dark crispy brown. This was really nice being with the family. Christmas has always been my best time of the year, especially since I've been in a position to give to my family. But the true gift of Christmas is being with the ones you really love and giving thanks for what you have. I'd been so blessed.

There will be plenty of gifts to open, and lots of love. What more could a person ask for? Freedom, maybe? Should I spend the next decade of Christmases behind bars, or will I be a free man riding horses bareback down uninhabited cocoanut tree-lined beaches of South America? The choice was mine, but I wanted my mother to feel it was hers.

"Mom, the house on Sunset is yours to do what you want with. Make sure Peanut gets the stereo and furniture. I want you and Sue to keep all the wood carvings. Oh, yeah, make sure Peanut gets the pickup, too. The Fast of Florida stock can be used as you guys need money. It's a hell of a company and has a great future."

"But Steve," she interrupted. "You're leaving us! I don't know what I'll do without you." I wasn't getting very far making Mom feel the decision was hers.

I put my arms around her, and continued, though this wasn't getting any easier. "Sue knows who to give my boats to. I'm leaving the bank account as it is—there's only a few grand in it—Mom, please don't cry, I'll be all right." I held her by her shoulders and looked her in the eyes. "Do you want to visit me the next ten Christmases behind walls and bars, or do you want to visit me on lush tropical islands where you've always dreamed to go?"

She smiled at that thought, then started crying again. "What about Sun Dog.? And Adidas? You love them so much. I can take Sunny, but I'm not taking care of that eagle! Feeding it rats and chickens! I'm not—"

"I'll come back for Sunny, and I'm giving Adidas to the Seabird Sanctuary. He'll get a good home there." I hugged her, and held her tight. My heart was pumping pain. All she could do was cry. When her tears finally stopped, she put her hands on my face and stared right into my soul.

"Steve, it's going to be hard with you gone, but I will feel much better knowing you are free, living as you want to. Thinking of you locked up would bring me more pain than to know you're just out of reach. I love you so much."

"I love you, too, Mom. I'll send for you and the girls and we'll meet in different countries. Don't worry. It's not over. Life has just begun. Mom, I've got some money under the drawers of your closet and in the laundry room. You know the spots. There's still a few bushes that are being fertilized in the yard. I'll tell you where, when I need them. Miguelito will be coming by to pick up different amounts of money at different times. I'll be in contact with you or have someone contact you so you'll know how much to give him. I have twenty-eight hundred grand in hundreds above the laundry room—"

"Twenty-eight hundred dollars?"

"No, Mom. Twenty-eight hundred *grand*. Two point eight million dollars."

"Oh my heavens, Stevie! Oh, my. Make sure you be careful, honey."

"I'm leaving you a few hundred grand that's in your room in the usual place, so you can get your hair done."

"Stop it, Stevie." She backed away and patted my cheek as she laughed. "You're so sweet. But I'd rather have you than all the money in the world."

"You will, Mom. Really. I want you to start enjoying life. You took care of us and were the best mom any kids could have. You have suffered enough and I don't want you suffering because I'm gone. Just remember, you'll be hearing from me plenty. I'll be like a ghost. I'll slip in to see you, right here in our own house. I just can't call you and let you know when I'm coming or going."

"Oh, honey, you'll be one ghost I'll be praying to see."

MIGUELITO AND I got together the first week of a new year, 1978. We flew to Key West, stayed at some friends' hotel, then flew back up to Miami and caught our plane to Caracas, Venezuela. I was 25 years old.

END

ACCORDING TO A 1983 article entitled "Tales of some who are citizens of the world" that appeared in the *St. Petersburg Times*, Steve Lamb was "one of Pinellas County's most renowned smugglers" and was being investigated in various states, including Michigan, North Carolina, New Mexico, and Nevada. It was also suggested in that same article that he had managed to sneak back into St. Pete Beach upon the death of his mother in 1981.

He hadn't; he'd sneaked in with his Venezuelan girlfriend, Jill, and spent time with his mother *before* she died.

ACKNOWLEDGMENTS

There are never enough good things to say about those who help in the convergence of pages that eventually become a book. Authors of true stories mine the memories of friends and relatives, the keen eyes and sage advice of editors, proof readers and booksellers, and the photo albums of others Who Were There. We were blessed with help from many, especially the following who are listed here alphabetically, without regard to hours or effort spent on our behalf. Each of them offered us exactly what we needed at the time we needed it. Thank you all, very, very much.

Billy Tess
Capt. Larry Blue
Dani Sherman
Doug Clouse (RIP)
Elizabeth Messer
Julie Rice
Nancy Frederich
Raymond Hinst
Raymond Hinst, III
Pat Barnes
Pat Daquanna
Susan D. Daquanna
Pete Goodrich
Ronda Burnham
Troy Polk
Yildred Tortosa Lamb

And a very special thank you to Trevor Hanson who has endured the highs and lows of this long journey. Through it all, his dedication and encouragment remained steadfast. He is truly a loyal friend, without whom this memoir may not have been made.

Steve Lamb and Diane Marcou

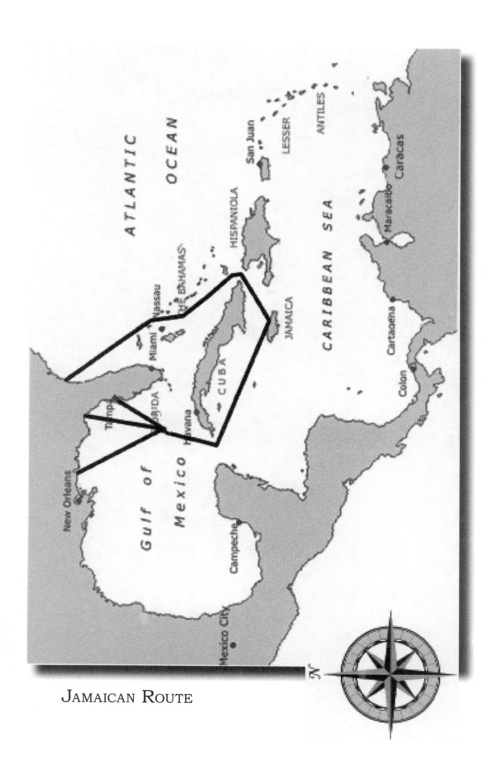

JAMAICAN ROUTE

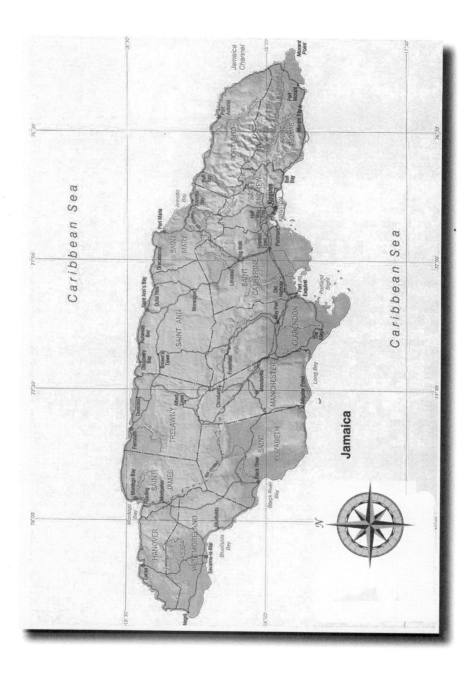

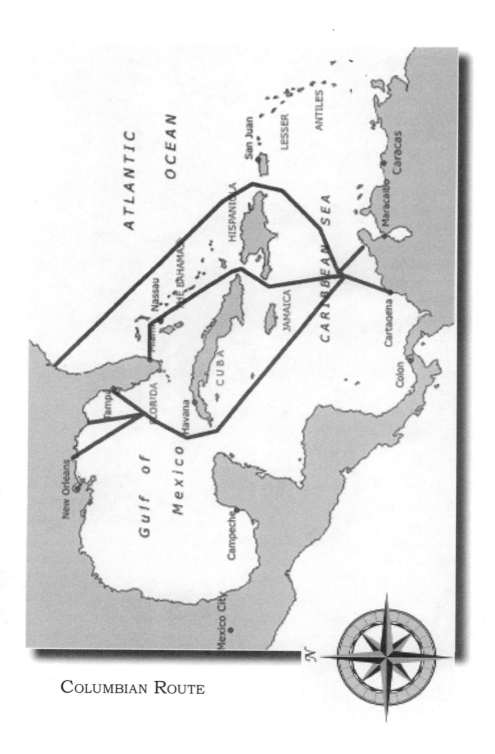

COLUMBIAN ROUTE

to be continued...

www.TheSmugglersGhost.com